MW00562173

Modern
Friendship

Also by Anna Goldfarb

Clearly, I Didn't Think This Through: The Story of One Tall Girl's Impulsive, Ill-Conceived, and Borderline Irresponsible Life Decisions

Modern Friendship

How to
Nurture Our
Most Valued
Connections

Anna Goldfarb

sounds true
BOULDER, COLORADO

Sounds True
Boulder, CO

© 2024 Anna Goldfarb

Sounds True is a trademark of Sounds True Inc.
All rights reserved. No part of this book may be used or reproduced in any manner without written permission from the author and publisher.

No AI Training: Without in any way limiting the author's and publisher's exclusive rights under copyright, any use of this publication to "train" generative artificial intelligence (AI) technologies to generate text is expressly prohibited. The author reserves all rights to license uses of this work for generative AI training and development of machine learning language models.

Some names and identifying details have been changed to protect the privacy of individuals.

Published 2024

Book design by Ranée Kahler

Printed in Canada

BK06828

Library of Congress Cataloging-in-Publication Data

Names: Goldfarb, Anna, author.
Title: Modern friendship : how to nurture our most valued connections / Anna
    Goldfarb.
Description: Boulder, CO : Sounds True, 2024. | Includes bibliographical references.
Identifiers: LCCN 2023042651 (print) | LCCN 2023042652 (ebook) |
    ISBN 9781649632081 (hardcover) | ISBN 9781649632128 (ebook)
Subjects: LCSH: Friendship--Sociological aspects. |
    Friendship--Psychological aspects.
Classification: LCC HM1161 .G65 2024 (print) | LCC HM1161 (ebook) |
    DDC 302.34--dc23/eng/20231102
LC record available at https://lccn.loc.gov/2023042651
LC ebook record available at https://lccn.loc.gov/2023042652

FSC
www.fsc.org
MIX
Paper | Supporting
responsible forestry
FSC® C016245

For my dad

Table of Contents

Introduction

In 2017, to better understand the dynamics swirling around me and learn the secret to comforting my friends who had increasingly more complex lives and problems, I began reporting on friendships, and what I found was alarmingly bleak. More than 300 million people on the planet don't have a single friend, according to recent Gallup data.[1]

As a journalist, I've written hundreds of pieces about relationships, communication, and mutual support for outlets like the *New York Times*, the *The Atlantic*, the *The Cut*, *TIME* magazine, and more. Those stories have been full of surprises, teaching me more than I ever could have expected to learn and connecting me with millions of readers who have confirmed that there's a real hunger for this knowledge. From a single woman in San Francisco who has struggled to maintain her friendship with her married friend in Los Angeles to a guy who moved to a new neighborhood with his fiancé and had no clue how to make new friends, there seems to be a prevailing pattern of "What is happening, and how the hell do I navigate this?" when it comes to friendships and relationships. The truth is, it's perfectly natural for friendships to mutate and decay in adulthood. But as common as this is, most people don't see it coming.

But don't just take my word for it. A 2016 study showed that after we turn twenty-five, our social circles naturally shrink.[2] Another study by sociologist Gerald Mollenhorst showed that we lose half of our close friends and replace them every seven years, on average.[3] HALF OF OUR CLOSE FRIENDS. EVERY SEVEN YEARS. SORRY FOR YELLING, BUT THAT'S JARRING.

However, it was seeing my father's apprehension to reconnect with a treasured childhood friend that made me realize there was something bigger, something more urgent, about demystifying our adult friendships. By understanding *why* we choose the friends we do—and who chooses *us* as their friends and why—we give our friendships the best chance to transform into beautiful, vibrant, flourishing relationships. These relationships are our legacy. They're how we leave a lasting imprint on the world.

In June 2020, I drove to my parents' house for a quick visit. It's a short drive over the Betsy Ross Bridge from my spot in Philly to their place in South Jersey. With the bright sun on our faces, my dad pulled up a chair and joined me on the back porch. The smell of fresh suburban lawn clippings tickled my nose. Since vaccines weren't available this early in the COVID-19 pandemic, visits to my parents were infrequent and always took place outside.

I had just written a piece for the *New York Times* about whether you should reach out to a friend you've lost touch with during lockdown. My thought was that if there was tension or conflict in your friendship, you might want to take a beat before popping up in their inbox unannounced.

Well, this piece opened an old wound within my dad's soul.

"After reading your article, I've been thinking a lot about Marty," he said. My dad couldn't pinpoint why he stopped talking to Marty, one of his close friends from childhood. He searched for answers but had none to give. The years of unexplained silence troubled him.

Since finding people's contact information online is my superpower, it took me five minutes to find Marty's details. I texted my dad Marty's email address, and I even wrote out a script for him to use: "Marty, you've been on my mind. I would love to catch up. Are you free on Tuesday or Wednesday to get on a call?"

The message was short and sweet. My goal was to make it easy for Marty to say "yes" to scheduling a call, considering they hadn't exchanged one syllable in more than fifteen years. I was used to solving friendship hiccups in my own life through my reporting, but this was the first time I was able to put my knowledge to use for my dad. I was flattered he asked me for help. Selfishly, I wanted a happy reconnection between them. My dad rarely approached me with interpersonal problems, so mending this rift made me feel like I could be his hero.

I pestered him every few weeks for an update: "Did you reach out to Marty yet?" Sadly, there wasn't an update to give. My dad never reached out to him. He didn't know how to explain his absence, he told me. What if Marty ignored his attempt at connection? Or he was angry at my father for abandoning their friendship? The uncertainty of the outcome—and the terror of rejection—rattled him.

In the end, they never connected. My father passed away six months after we had this conversation. Between Christmas and New Year's Day, my dad contracted a severe infection in his hip. Five days after being discharged from the hospital, he tested positive for COVID-19. His body, exhausted from fighting the bacterial infection, had no gas left in the tank. At 5 am on a brisk Sunday in January 2021, my sister woke me up to let me know my dad's situation was dire. He was about to be moved from a CPAP machine to a ventilator. She told me I should FaceTime him to, essentially, say goodbye. It was unfathomable that none of us could be with him. Through the screen, I told him, "Rest. Let your body heal," over and over again. "I love you, Dad." He was unable to reply as the CPAP machine whirred so he gave me a thumbs-up to let me know my message was received.

After we ended the call, I texted him: "I love you so much. Thank you for every sacrifice you made. I couldn't ask for a better dad." I don't know if he read it.

Later that morning, as the sunlight grew strong and the day found its footing, his heart—my favorite heart in the universe, the metronome whose powerful thump I felt throb with every bear hug he gave me—stopped beating.

Everything about my dad's death was unthinkable. My dad—the silliest, smartest, friendliest person I knew, who collected friends like some people collect Beanie Babies—had four people at his funeral: me, my sister, my husband, and my mom. We were still weeks away from a COVID vaccine, and none of his four grandkids were able to attend. My older sister in Boston watched an online feed of our father's coffin being lowered into the frigid ground with her husband and daughter at her side. We buried our dad, then headed home to process our heartbreak alone.

My family was in crisis mode precisely when the entire planet was in crisis mode too. There wasn't a soft place to land. The pain of my dad's passing was unreal. In this fog of sadness and shock, my mind kept returning to Marty.

The day after the funeral, I reached out to Marty's son on LinkedIn. I asked him to put me in touch with his father. Forty-five minutes later, I was on the phone with my dad's long-lost best friend.

Marty seemed pleased to hear from me. "Hello, Anna!"

"Is this a good time to talk?" I asked, surprising myself with my ability to keep my composure. "Are you somewhere quiet? Are you sitting down?" He assured me he was.

"Oh, Marty." My voice wavered, getting caught in my throat. "My dad passed away two days ago."

He gasped.

"My dad wanted to reach out to you last summer," I told him. "We had an entire conversation about how he wanted to connect with you, but—"

"It's not his fault," Marty said. "I have responsibility here too. I could've reached out to him just as easily as he could've reached out to me."

As the news of my dad's passing settled in, Marty shared a few funny stories about what my dad was like growing up in Queens. How they attended high school football games together. And how they both annoyed my grandma by tracking mud in her house with their sneakers.

Through tears, Marty thanked me for reaching out to him. I invited him to my dad's online *shiva* later that evening. Seeing him in the ocean of faces and names there to remember my father felt like healing. It felt like closure.

I gave Marty the gift of knowing with certainty that he—and their friendship—mattered to my father. If I shut my eyes, I could see my dad saying "thank you" to me.

After that experience with Marty, I knew I had to write this book. I don't think my dad had many regrets in his life, but having this distance from his oldest friend haunted him. It doesn't have to be this way. I don't want anyone to carry the burden of crippling, anxious fear, especially when it comes to something as essential as our friendships.

I've been reporting on different facets of friendship for years, but with this book, I wanted to put together something bigger, a manual so you don't have to second-guess or talk yourself out of finding connection with the most meaningful people in your life.

Your friendships are precious. They're vital. *They matter.* So let's understand, cultivate, and harness their incredible power. Yes, it feels fantastic to know you have people to rely on, who are essential to your life. But it feels even more marvelous to know that your friends appreciate you for your inner beauty and strong character too. And that when all is said and done, when we look back on the contours of our lives, we can know with certainty that we—and our cherished friends—were valuable.

I'm not a life coach or a psychologist, and I'm definitely not a wellness guru. I'm a journalist, and as part of my work, I talk to experts, academics, and researchers to see what everyone is missing about the whole modern friendship thing. In this book, I will share what I've learned with you so we all can apply it to our lives.

Simply because I'm writing this book, you might think I'm a superstar poster child of a friend, but let me stop you right there. I'm *not* a perfect friend. For instance, I still offer unhelpful advice all the goddamn time. In fact, this exact conversation happened last week:

Me: to a friend stressed out by the amount of laundry she needs to do: Have you tried throwing money at the problem? Maybe hiring someone to do your laundry?
Friend (sarcastically): Geez. I haven't thought of that, Anna.

But now I know better. I can recover equilibrium quicker and remove the sting faster.

Me: Ooof. Sorry about my thoughtless comment. It was probably annoying for me to act like I know your problems better than you do.

Friend (relieved): It's fine. Maybe I can ask my fantasy personal secretary to hire a person to do my laundry. Just have an entire staff dedicated to doing my laundry. That sounds like an efficient solution.

Me (sympathetically): Let's try this again. Laundry sucks. I'm happy to come over and help you fold clothes later today if you'd like.

Face saved.

I can't promise I can make you a perfect friend, so let's just get that out of the way too. I can, however, teach you how to be a *better* friend. A calmer friend. A more confident, secure friend. Because when we make mistakes with our friends (which we totally, absolutely, 100 percent will), you will feel empowered to know you have the skills to correct course quickly and build your friendship on even steadier ground.

Modern friendship isn't just about sipping Chardonnay with your bestie like an Instagram ad for a cashmere poncho. Instead, modern friendship is about the story you tell yourself about why a friend didn't respond to your text message asking if they wanted to get together this week for dinner. It's experiencing the specific pain of knowing you have best friends but they live across the country and you have no idea when you'll see them again. It's about knowing why some of your friendships feel life-affirming, while others feel like an unpleasant job you'd prefer to quietly quit. Friendships take on many shapes and sizes and are constantly evolving. This book is a tool to help you set realistic expectations and periodically check in and diagnose these changes.

In part 1 of the book, I'll teach you why you have the friends you do, then help you identify what parts of the relationship are in your control and which aren't. If you're feeling like you're swimming in strange waters alongside your friend, you definitely are. It's not your imagination; friendship norms are changing rapidly, and it's . . . a lot to wrap one's head around. Our parents and grandparents didn't have social media apps or smartphones when they were our age. If their friends drifted away, they couldn't open an app to see their friends alive and well, hanging out with other people. The way we engage in friendships today is kind of wild (and definitely not normal) when you think about it.

In part 2, I will teach you how to be a better friend and give your favorite friendships the best chance to thrive, how to be a person your friends seek out, and how to enjoy your time with these people. And in part 3, I will share practical tips, exercises, prompts, and advice on how to make time for your friendships when life revs up. You get busy. Other people get busy. Pets get sick. Work gets demanding. Friendships often take a back seat when calendars get full. But there are strategies you can use to maintain regular contact with your chosen inner circle.

Being an adult in a busy, stressful, and chaotic world is harder than tweezing your eyebrows while jumping on a trampoline. That's the paradox of adult friendships: when we feel too weak or broken to tend to our friendships in the way we'd like, that's precisely when we need our friends the most.

By the end of the book, you're going to be a friendship dynamo! All the time you'd spend worrying about whether you're a good friend or not will be replaced with the confidence of knowing that you're a fabulous friend who approaches adult friendships with realistic expectations and a confident attitude. You will be able to pinpoint who exactly is in your inner circle and come away with an actionable game plan for making your existing friendships work for you.

Throughout the book, I mostly use feminine pronouns (she/her) to refer to friends. This is merely to streamline things. All of what I cover applies to any gender identity. I've also changed the names of the dozens of people mentioned throughout to protect their privacy. You may notice I don't give a lot of individual details on these people whose anecdotes pepper the book. What matters is the truth and vulnerability of their experiences. I wanted their stories to be a chorus adding richness and depth to the conversation.

Reflect on the exercises. Incorporate small tweaks into your words, thoughts, and actions. Always be open to improvement. And have some fun while you're at it.

Three months after we buried my dad, we needed to design a headstone for his grave. The nice lady at the cemetery asked my family what wording we'd like to use, but none of us had ever written a headstone before.

Ever the journalist, my instinct was to research the appropriate verbiage. The following week, I visited my dad's grave and looked around. The wording on the headstones sounded official: father, mother, grandfather, grandmother. Long words. Formal sounding.

Huh, I thought. *I would never call my dad* father. *He always signed* Pops *on his grandchildren's birthday cards, never* grandfather. In my (admittedly unscientific) survey of the cemetery, I didn't see one headstone where the deceased was ever described as a friend.

My dad was so many things to so many people: a surfer who loved cats, a scientist and a professor, a volunteer referee for the Special Olympics. It didn't feel right to label him with stuffy words he wouldn't have chosen for himself. No, I wanted to describe my father using the words we knew him as. Then it came to me:

LOVING HUSBAND, DAD, POPS, AND FRIEND

"That's the headstone," I told my mom and sisters. "That's what I want it to say." They agreed. That's what we went with. That's who he was to us. That's who he was to the world. I'd like to think my dad would be pleased with that inscription.

We've all had our social lives upended in the wake of the pandemic, so now is the perfect time to reflect on what worked before, what didn't, and what we can do to make our favorite friendships stronger. Now, go be a friend to the most awesome people you can find.

PART 1

WHO MATTERS TO US

1

Modern Friendship Is Wild

During the 1936 Summer Olympics, there was a three-way tie for second place in the men's pole vault event.[1] A jump-off would determine which of the three competitors would win the silver and bronze medals. The first vaulter, an American named Bill Sefton, tried and failed to better his score. He was eliminated, so it came down to a pair of Japanese pole vaulters, Shuhei Nishida and Sueo Ōe, who were good friends. In a move that astonished everyone, they declined to compete against each other. Instead, they chose to share the honor.

After a long discussion, Japanese officials decided to award the silver medal to Nishida and the bronze medal to Ōe, based on their previous jump attempts. Nishida and Ōe weren't stoked with this result. In another surprising twist, upon their return to Japan, the two competitors cut their medals in half and welded them together. They each received a half-silver, half-bronze medal and called these black-and-white-cookie-esque medallions the "Medals of Friendship."

Can we talk about how punk rock it is to cut an Olympic medal in half and fuse it with another Olympic medal? Bad. Ass.

This friendship sounds so pure and uncomplicated and clearly more important to both men than recognition for their athletic achievements.

It sounds almost like a fable, a story Danny Tanner would tell DJ while sitting on the edge of her bed after she's quarreled with Kimmy Gibbler.

Part of me is jealous to hear this tale of friendship triumph. This account looks nothing like my friendships today. I barely have time to see my friends, much less find myself in a situation where I can make a dramatic gesture involving a soldering gun. It's challenging enough to agree on when and where we can meet up for a cup of too-strong coffee. Most of my closest friends have moved away physically, either across town or across the country. Or they have moved away emotionally, into new roles as spouses, parents, aunties, uncles, and caretakers. The more things you are to more people, the more precious your free time is. My friends' time, for the most part, is already spoken for, so as a result, I'm competing against their work commitments, significant others, children, pets, grocery shopping, laundry, and workouts for some good old-fashioned face time.

When we do connect, there's so much to catch up on that it's baffling to know where to start. *How's your job? How's your family? What are your thoughts on the latest episode of* Housewives of Somewhere Fancier and Warmer Than Where We Live?

Our conversations, if we have them over the phone or in person, can feel jagged and lurching. I get overly nervous: *Does she want to talk about her child's recent autism diagnosis? Am I asking intrusive questions about her marriage? How am I supposed to respond when she complains about her husband for the trillionth time? Am I annoying her with my rants about my craptastic boss?* Why isn't this easier?

I've reached out to say, "Hey, girl! Just thinking of you."

I've texted, "I miss your face. Can we get together soon, please?"

I've followed up when I haven't heard back.

I've felt like a borderline pest: "Did you see my messages? Just making sure they're not in your spam folder lol."

I've made excuses for their silences: *Maybe they're slammed at work. Maybe they're too busy with schoolwork. Maybe their depression is back. Maybe, maybe, maybe.*

I've liked countless social media posts of my friends' silly, floppy children and their fuzzy pets. I've commented, "Looks delish!" on their poorly lit photos of freshly baked sourdough bread and the random baked feta pasta dish from a viral TikTok recipe.

None of this has made me feel like I'm making a real connection with my cherished friends. And it comes to a point where I sometimes feel as though I don't have any cherished friends at all.

Emma's Experience

Emma told me she gets hundreds of messages on her birthday every year on social media but didn't know who to text when her mom got into a car accident. "It just didn't feel like it was in the nature of my relationships to burden my friends with a personal issue," she told me. The experience left her reeling because even the people who knew her best weren't in a position to give her support when she needed it.

This strange paradox of knowing you have close friends but feeling, simultaneously, that you don't have any close friends is a familiar feeling that encapsulates the entire modern friendship sphere. The vast majority of us in Western society have unprecedented selection in who we can befriend across genders, races, and class backgrounds. Unlike our ancestors, we're not limited as much by place and time, thanks to our cheap, plentiful ease of communication. But the trade-off to all this choice is that we're more likely to have disparate friend groups. There's little cohesion: you have friends from school, friends from work, and friends who share your hobbies and passions. They might only have history and commonality with you, not with each other.

Modernity believes in equality, individualism, choice, self-expression, and freedom, so our friendships naturally reflect those values, said author and essayist William Deresiewicz in the *The Chronicle for Higher Education*.[2] "The modern temper runs toward unrestricted fluidity and flexibility, the endless play of possibility, and so is perfectly suited to the informal, improvisational nature of friendship," he wrote. "We can be friends with whomever we want, however we want, for as long as we want." That's the beauty and burden of modern friendship in a nutshell.

It's not our fault that our friendships are becoming harder to maintain. But it is our responsibility to understand the new modern friendship landscape and find ways to establish connection with other people. It's on us to educate ourselves about how to be a friend to others because society is not going to make it easy for us. Modern friendship is about choice, time, and attention because modern life is all about:

1. **How you choose to spend your time.** We all have the same amount of time in a given day. How we decide to use those hours, minutes, and seconds matters. Being intentional about maintaining our friendships is a choice we can all make. We can choose to deepen our friendships just as easily as we can choose to let friendships drift.

2. **What you give your attention to.** Harnessing your attention is a superpower. It's basically like flying or being invisible but *waaaaay* less dangerous. Noticing changes in our friends' lives—challenging medical issues, sensitive financial issues, turbulent emotional issues—will deepen the relationship in incredible ways.

For example, if you pay attention to the fact that your friend recently went vegan, you can suggest places to grab lunch that have vegan food. This, in turn, will make it easier for your friend to say yes to your lunch invitation. If your friend recently lost their job, you can suggest grabbing a slice of pizza for dinner instead of an elaborate (and pricey) sushi feast. If your friend is depressed, you'll know to give them some leeway when it takes a few days for them to return a call. The beauty of attention is that it's free to give, and it makes your friends feel noticed, valued, and loved.

When you don't fully listen, you will miss opportunities to be useful and helpful to those you love, but when you pay attention to the right things, you will notice more ways to make yourself helpful. And when your friends fully listen to you, they will find ways to reciprocate, and you will actually enjoy the friendships you have.

Most people focus on the wrong aspects in their friendships, spending too much time criticizing themselves for not knowing how to perfectly manage these bonds. They don't give enough thought to what they say to their friends to support them when they do actually connect. They also talk themselves out of pursuing connection. People, for the most part, don't know how to communicate disappointment or give reassurance. They also don't make their friendships feel fun.

Finally, most people take things *so personally*. They don't give their friends the benefit of the doubt and jump straight to offense when, often, there is none there to begin with.

We live in a complex, busy society, but we expect our friendships to fall into place wordlessly without negotiation. This entire system and approach sets us up for failure.

I *wish* cementing my friendships could be as simple as gluing two medals together. That sounds like a dream because it's both a statement to the larger world and to each other. This medal-smooshing wasn't contrived either. It wasn't for Instagram or to increase engagement or boost their personal brand. No, it was simple. Direct. Meaningful.

The reality is that friendships in adulthood are endangered. Studies show that after thirty, it's both more challenging to foster new friendships and harder to renegotiate old ones.[3] It can feel like you're stuck between forging new bonds from scratch or feeling beholden to people and patterns you've outgrown. There's only so much we can do in a given day to nurture our friendships when work and family obligations need our immediate attention.

It's understandable, but it's also concerning because friendships are essential to our emotional and physical well-being. They make good times exponentially more awesome and bad times infinitely more bearable.

In fact, according to a study by Julianne Holt-Lunstad, an associate psychology professor at Brigham Young University, a solid social network can boost your longevity by as much as 50 percent and be as beneficial as kicking a fifteen-cigarette-a-day smoking habit.[4] Your real-life social network can be "more important to physical health than exercising or beating obesity," Holt-Lunstad concluded.

WHY ADULT FRIENDSHIPS ARE HARD TO ACHIEVE

If we continue to think of friendships the way we did as children, we may be under the impression that they're effortless to cultivate and maintain, and perhaps, in a perfect world, this could be the case. But unfortunately, in this fractured modern landscape we find ourselves in, with the responsibilities and obligations adulthood bestows upon us, achieving and maintaining friendships can feel like pushing a Volvo uphill while wearing flip-flops.

I'm here to reassure you that there are valid reasons why you may feel this way and that you are not alone in this struggle. Let's uncover a few of them.

Factor #1: Society Isn't Set Up to Support Adult Friendships

I hate to drop some bad news on you so early in the book, but as a society we're experiencing a troubling friendship crisis. Americans report talking to friends less often and relying on friends less for personal support, according to a May 2021 survey by the American Enterprise Institute's American Perspectives.[5] The reasons given:

People are getting married later in life.

raises hand I was married at thirty-nine years old, which is basically ancient compared to my mother, who married at twenty-one, and my grandmother, who married at eighteen. Getting married later in life meant that my husband and I had completely separate friendship circles when we met. It's pretty difficult (if not impossible) to combine friend groups at this stage in the game. At least for me, it's been a challenge. We do have another child-free couple in our neighborhood that we go on double dates with, so it's been an easy fit there. But when it comes to maintaining friendships with the people we met before we got together, we often spend time with them on our own. This approach takes time away from our marriage, so I have to be selective with the friends I do meet up with.

People are more mobile than ever.

raises hand again I've lived, worked, and attended school in three major cities (Chicago, New York City, and Philadelphia) over the past twenty years. Most of my friends from childhood and young adulthood don't live near me. One friend is in San Francisco, another is in St. Louis, and another is in Richmond, Virginia. It's tough to keep the flame of friendship lit when you don't see each other often, if at all. And as the last few years have shown us, if we don't make an effort to keep in contact with our loved ones, bonds will decay.

Parents are spending twice as much time with their children than previous generations.

This means they have less time to pursue and maintain friendships. I'm not a parent, but a lot of my friends are. I know how valuable their downtime is and how essential it is that they recharge at the end of the day. It's a shame our connection might suffer because of their new role as parents, but it's totally understandable if they can't gab on the phone after putting (multiple!) children to bed. I get it. And I accept it. But it doesn't mean it hasn't been a wobbly transition to accept that my friends' availability has shifted.

People are working longer hours and traveling more for work.

When it comes to making a living, friendships are often first on the chopping block when we're pressed for time. *raises hand yet again* As a freelance journalist, I often work crazy hours—sometimes nights and weekends. Work pays my bills and, well, friendships don't. So it can feel difficult to prioritize friendships that, on the surface, don't seem to contribute to my household's bottom line. I probably sound like a cold-blooded capitalist, but I'm just keeping it real!

These sweeping, widespread sociological trends are bigger than you or me, showing just how our generation behaves that makes holding on to friendships exhausting.

Factor #2: Trust in Others Is at an All-Time Low

We live in a fractured society that distrusts one another, and our strained friendships are a reflection of our deeply dysfunctional society. Public trust in the government sits at near-historic lows today, according to a 2019 Pew Research Center poll.[6] Confidence levels in newspapers, the three branches of government, organized religion, the criminal justice system, corporations, and the police are all declining. Only around one-tenth of respondents are satisfied with the way things are going in the country right now. That's dismal!

This rise of mistrust has trickled down to palpable mistrust among our fellow citizens too. According to a 2019 report on Trust and Distrust in America, 71 percent of those surveyed thought interpersonal confidence in other Americans had worsened in the past twenty years.[7] Half of those surveyed said their fellow Americans were not as reliable as they used to be.

My grandparents knew everyone on their street in suburban Philadelphia, and as I write this, I don't even know my next-door neighbors' names. All I know is that the woman across the hall has an anime sticker on her Honda Element, and her boyfriend has a shaved head. End of list.

This lack of trust in our communities affects our ability to form friendships with one another because friendships require mutual vulnerability where each person feels safe expressing their true selves. Without a baseline of trust, people are less likely to let down their guard, which makes establishing a genuine connection with potential friends less likely. If you move through life assuming betrayal or disappointment is around the corner, you'll never put yourself in a position to allow friendships to organically form.

Factor #3: Your Personality Quirks Make It Harder to Make and Keep Friends

According to researchers Menelaos Apostolou and Despoina Keramari, there are two personality traits that reduce one's capacity to make friends: high introversion and low trust. In a 2020 paper published in the *Personality and Individual Differences* journal, the researchers explained this was due to two reasons:[8]

Introverts enjoy solitary pursuits, which decrease their opportunities to meet new people.

Friendships are like sending a rover to Mars, in that they take a long time to make happen. If you aren't putting yourself in situations where you're spending long stretches of time with others, friendships are less likely to take hold. If you like playing a team sport like kickball, you need to find other people to play kickball with. But if you like playing solitary games like Wordle, well, you don't need a team of people to get in on that.

If you're an extrovert, you're more likely to make time for socializing. Therefore, you will put yourself in a position to meet new people more often. My dad was a classic extrovert, partially because he had so many interests that required other people to be in the room. He played recreational squash at the University of Pennsylvania, golf at his local country club, and he loved refereeing basketball at local high schools and racing cars in Watkins Glen in Upstate New York. Because his interests required other people to participate alongside him, he had bushels of friends from all walks of life.

On the flip side, my older sister loved learning about the power of crystals and the practice of Reiki, which are both solitary-ish pursuits. It wasn't until she joined a running club in Boston a few years ago—shout-out to the Shamrocks—that her social network exploded. Now she volunteers at races and runs marathons with an army of support around her. Embracing activities that require others positioned her to cultivate community.

If your passion is watching rom-coms, solving crossword puzzles (in pen!), or taking long walks listening to *This American Life*, you're not going to naturally meet other people, as you aren't putting yourself in a position to do so.

Studies show it takes about two hundred hours over the course of a few months to promote someone from the "stranger" category into the "close friend" category.[9] That's a lot of time together, which is easy to rack up when you live in the same dorm or work in adjacent cubicles. If you aren't naturally spending long stretches of time around others, finding those hundreds of hours will be a challenge.

Some people are slow to trust new people.

Researchers call the ability to trust others *agreeableness*. When you're high in agreeableness, you cooperate with others, afford people the benefit of the doubt, and generally assume that most people are fundamentally good at their core. Not everyone regards others in this way, though.

"Some people trust others easily, while other people are more suspicious of others," Drs. Apostolou and Keramari wrote in a 2020 study.[10] "Individuals who score low in trust may face difficulties in making friends because even if they meet people who could potentially become their friends, they may not give them a chance to be so."[11] If you're prickly or hesitant to people who reach out to you, you may never stick around long enough to forge those deeper friendships you crave.

In *Sesame Street* terms, if you're an extroverted Big Bird brimming with agreeableness, you're going to make friends with everyone in the neighborhood. But if you're giving introverted Oscar the Grouch vibes, you will find making friends more challenging.

Factor #4: Friendships Can Collapse for Interpersonal Reasons

According to *Psychology Today*, the five most common reasons friendships become strained are:[12]

A move. Whether it's across town or across the country, moves disrupt routines, shift priorities, and make closeness tough to achieve.

A mismatch in values or opinions. You realize your politics are incompatible. You sense your friend isn't as committed to dismantling racism as you are. You value making wise financial decisions, and your friend is frivolous with their money. Whatever the reason, you two aren't on the same page about something important. This makes the time you do spend together feel fraught or draining.

A change in life circumstances outside one's control. Illness, loss, marriage, divorce, parenthood, job loss, bankruptcy—the list goes on and on. All of these events influence the circle of support a person seeks out. Not every friendship is equipped to handle these events or changes, and you may feel surprised or hurt that your friends aren't able to be there for you in the way you require. It's not that they're bad people; they're just unequipped to help you navigate the problems you're facing.

A conflict of some sort. This speaks to any betrayal, malicious action, or egregious violation of trust, like a friend hooking up with your ex, stealing from you, or bad-mouthing you.

A change in personality or lifestyle. You might still be physically close to one another, but existentially, you're in two different places. This happens all the time in middle school, as kids figure out who they are and try on different labels and identities. For instance, someone might realize they're goth and only want to hang out with the other goth kids to talk about black lipstick and Trent Reznor, so they move on from their previous friend group. This happens in adulthood too. A newly sober friend might feel uncomfortable seeking out her hard-partying former friends. And a friend embracing religion may only seem interested in socializing with people in her new church.

It's possible a friendship might wane due to a combination of these issues, which can make the relationship feel even more tenuous. Perhaps you have a friend who has moved six states away *and* adopted extremist political views. Well, you don't need a Magic 8 Ball to see that the odds of maintaining closeness are not so good.

Looking at this comprehensive list of why friendships deteriorate brings up a range of feelings for me. I'd always assumed my friendships were magical and unique, so it's strange to see the reasons for my shaky bonds encapsulated in such a concise way.

It's like when your car's battery light goes off and you take your car to a mechanic to assess what's causing the issue. It never occurred to me to treat my friendships like wonky cars or misbehaving electronics. But that's exactly what we're doing. We're diagnosing what went wrong.

We've spent some time discussing the widespread sociological reasons, personality hiccups, and situation-specific reasons friendships decay. Next, we add our own brains to the mix, which show up with a litany of excuses as to why we might resist investing in friendships. In her book *We Should Get Together: The Secret to Cultivating Better Friendships*, author Kat Vellos's research uncovered dozens of reasons why adults deprioritize friendship. A few of the big ones are:

- Availability issues: "I'm too busy to see my friends."

- Career concerns: "I'd rather use my free time to develop myself professionally and build my career."

- Priorities: "My family and/or romantic relationships need to come first right now."

- Lifestyle preferences: "I'd rather use my free time to relax alone."

- Health concerns: "I'd rather use my free time to exercise and get in shape."

- Financial worries: "I make a lot less, or a lot more, than my friends, and that creates a strain on our relationships."

- Exhaustion: "I don't have the energy to invest in friendships right now."

- Physical distance challenges: "I've moved away and don't know anyone. Or, my friends have moved away from me."

- Emotional challenges: "I've had friends betray me, so I'm wary about letting people into my life."

If you've been looking at your schedule and have decided that spending time connecting with friends is low on your list, I hear you. Who among us hasn't let out a groan when you receive a text from a friend right as you settle in to watch a movie? Or when a friend invites you over for a drink right after you've unhooked your bra? Sure, friendships can feel inconvenient. You might even resent having to manage these requests at connection. You might think, *God, replying to this friend is one more thing I have to do. When does this shit end? When can I just worry about me and not everyone else on the planet?* Even the healthiest friendships require sacrifice. It necessitates putting ourselves second from time to time. That might feel annoying or uncomfortable, especially if you aren't 100 percent enthusiastic about the person you're doing all this sacrificing for.

I want to be clear: there is nothing wrong with you and your capacity to hold on to your friendships. What's wrong is that our society is not setting us up for success when it comes to maintaining these friendships. We live in a hyper-fluid culture where we can change jobs, residences, and even our own identities, oftentimes without any friction. It's not just your imagination; we have new forces pulling us in new directions (more on the impact of these trends in chapter 3). Even though we can move through groups, communities, and cliques with ease, all these changes impact our intimate bonds. Looking back at my own life—sliding between the punk rock scene in Chicago to the indie rock music scene in New York City to the dance party scene in Philly to being a boring middle-aged wife in my forties—each of these moves left some friends behind.

But we should still push through and create space for our friends because our lives will get better in every conceivable way when we have wonderful friends who matter to us. Because when we talk about friendship, we're really talking about two things: (1) how to find people who matter to us, and (2) how to matter to the people we love and admire.

Modern friendship puts us in a precarious position because we don't need to rely on our neighbors and friends the same way our parents and grandparents did. This is the consequence of having information available to us instantaneously. I don't need to ask my neighbor with the shaved head what the loud bang was on the street because my inbox is clogged with Nextdoor posts of neighbors sharing that exact information. I don't need to ask my neighbor how to change a car tire; I can watch a YouTube video about how to do it. I don't need to ask a friend what the soreness in my hands could be; I've already Googled it and diagnosed myself. (I played video games on my Nintendo Switch for too long, and my hands weren't happy with that decision.)

So our modern friendship challenge is figuring out how to stay connected when information is cheap and plentiful. What can we offer one another that a Google search can't? Well, it comes down to human stuff, like sympathy, empathy, and compassion. A YouTube video doesn't care how I feel about having to change a car tire (I imagine I'd feel self-pity), but other humans can care about people and let them know they matter to us, which is valuable in this attention economy.

Technology will never make us feel like we matter. That our uniqueness, sense of humor, and integrity matter. That's why technology will always come up short. Engaging with it will never be as fulfilling as spending time with a cherished friend. It simply can't compare. Our brains know the difference between Facebook wishing us happy birthday and our dear friends wishing us happy birthday.

We all spend our time on what matters to us. And friendship is a specialized accounting of this time: the people you yearn to spend your time with, the people you prioritize spending your time with, and the people you actually enjoy spending your time with. Ideally, we want to spend high-quality time with our favorite high-quality friends regularly. But, in practice, we rarely do.

Additionally, friendship is a story of our time spent exploring the world together and for how long:

- "I've known Brian since kindergarten. I was a best man at his wedding last year."

- "Alanna and I met at camp in fifth grade."

- "I met Zoe the first day of college in 2003. We ended up getting an apartment together when we graduated."

- "Paige and I met at work eight years ago."

It's finding ways to spend your time together in the future:

- "Chrissy? We're in the same book club. I see her every third Thursday of the month."

- "I'm in a pottery class with Marco. We signed up together."
- "Want to join a softball league with me? We meet on Tuesday nights."
- "I just booked a girls' getaway trip to Atlantic City next month. You're coming, right?"
- "One day when we retire, we're going to be two old biddies playing mah-jongg in the retirement home. I already have my muumuu picked out."

It's prioritizing spending time together:

- "I should reach out to Danny this week."
- "Let's invite Betsy over for dinner on Sunday."
- "I haven't heard from Jesse in a minute. I'm going to invite him out to coffee."

It's asking them to hang out with you:

- "Any interest in watching the new Marvel movie with me? We can go to that theater with the reclining seats."
- "Come over to my house. Let's have iced tea on the patio. I want to hear all about your vacation."
- "I need to return some clothes to the Gap. Want to come along with me? We can get Shake Shack afterward."

And it's about loving the time you spend together:

- "You always know what to say to lighten my mood."
- "You feel like family to me."
- "Thanks for listening to me. You're so good at making me feel validated."

- "I always feel so good seeing you."

- "I wish we could spend the entire day together just shootin' the shit."

Friendship is the sum total of the decisions you made in the past, the choices you make today, and the things you plan for in the future. These small daily choices show our high-quality friends what matters to us, which in turn will help them do the same.

Discovering who those high-quality friends are can be a bit challenging at first, but I've found that there are six no-nonsense truths of modern friendships that can demystify them and lift the weight of intimidation off your shoulders.

2

Six Hard Truths about Modern Friendship

Sometimes I wish I had someone in my life who could've sat me down and explained how and why friendships drift apart. I certainly didn't know anyone in my life who had these things figured out.

When I was a teenager growing up on the North Shore of Chicago, my friendships were simpler, partly because of circumstance. After a childhood spent zigzagging across the country (by the age of fifteen, I had attended eight schools in three cities), I was a professional new kid in class. I watched other kids enjoy long-standing friendships with peers they had known since their days playing tag on the playground. I couldn't compete with that history. I was the (untested) new brand of salsa on the shelf; why pick me when you already had your favorite jar of Old El Paso?

Nervous about rejection, it felt safer to wait for other kids to engage me. I had no strategy for how to initiate plans with classmates who looked promising. I didn't know myself well enough to even suggest something I'd want to do with a friend. I couldn't drive. My house wasn't ideal for entertaining, so I definitely wasn't inviting a friend over. I also had no money. What could we do? Go for a walk in the neighborhood? Loiter at a local playground?

I did have an inkling that music could be my way into connection. One bubbly girl in my eighth grade class named Penelope loved exactly two things: the Chicago Bulls and the Red Hot Chili Peppers. She seemed like a promising friend because she always smiled at me when we crossed paths in the hall. We sat next to each other on a class field trip to D.C., and she laughed at my jokes.

I just needed to create an opening, something to really show her that I would be a great friend candidate. That weekend, I took the bus to the mall a half hour away and purchased the *Blood Sugar Sex Magik* cassette. The following Monday, I made sure to flash the tape when Penelope walked by my locker.

"No way! *You* like the Red Hot Chili Peppers?" she asked, delighted. "They're my favorite band!"

"No way!" I replied, mirroring her language. I feigned surprise at the coincidence. "I'm a huge fan. I can't believe you love this band too."

Ultimately, my gambit worked. She ended up becoming my best friend that year. Yes, I felt like a pickup artist using smoke and mirrors to manufacture interest on her part, but hey, I really did like the song "Under the Bridge." I like to think I was being strategic about making new friends instead of creepily manipulating the moment, but honestly, it was probably a mixture of both.

Once forged, maintaining friendships during my childhood was just . . . *easier*. Even my strongest friendships required little effort; I showed up at the same places (school, another friend's house) and enjoyed the same things as my friends (punk rock bands, Taco Bell bean-and-cheese burritos). When I moved to New York City in 1996 to attend college, I essentially did the same thing. I gravitated toward the artsy, rebellious kids. We'd slink around indie rock shows at the Knitting Factory, attend our friends' art openings, and try (and let's be real, mostly fail) to hook up with attractive people.

Being best friends meant we both hated each other's ex-boyfriends and our crappy postcollege jobs. Friendship seemed simple, for the most part. My friends and I didn't have much money, but we were flush with free time, and our hangouts were endless.

This all started to change once I reached my mid- to late twenties. My friendships frayed as expectations, priorities, and circumstances shifted.

Loyalty to each other was great, but it wasn't enough to sustain a bumpy friendship. Friends moved away. Some got married. Some had children. Then I moved to Philadelphia in 2002 and had to build a new social network from scratch. I didn't have a road map to help me or my friends navigate these changes.

Interpersonal problems bubbled up—jealousy, envy, abandonment— and we didn't have the vocabulary to address it. I learned I was fantastic at confronting the world with my buddies side by side, hip to hip, but I was useless at handling matters when things got sticky between us. I had no clue what to say when I let someone down or how to tell a friend she had hurt my feelings. Resentments piled up. Silences turned into permanent chills.

I was not prepared to weather these challenges on any level. No one in my orbit could explain what was happening. My parents and grandparents weren't much help, as they had little experience cultivating friendships with people of other genders or diverse backgrounds. None of my peers had much perspective to give either; they were just as clueless as I was. All we could do was commiserate: *Things are tough and weird, and I wish I could help you, but this is above my pay grade.*

Friendship breakups are excruciating. When you break up with a significant other, people are quick to extend compassion, but when you break up with a friend, there's no way to categorize that grief. It's lonely. And embarrassing.

The person you'd normally lean on to process the pain is now the one person who's off limits to approach. The pain of a friendship breakup can vibrate in the background for years, never clicking off.

It can be hard to separate from a friend, especially one you've made many positive memories with. But we are all human, and we will make mistakes. These rifts in friendships are inevitable, but they don't have to spell disaster. Now that I've become well acquainted with this friendship topic, I'm in the position to gently tell you (as an older sister or favorite cousin) these six hard truths about modern friendships. If you keep these truths in mind, you'll set yourself up to have successful relationships that don't deny your friends their humanness. Grab a seat; these might sting a little.

TRUTH #1: FRIENDS WILL DISAPPOINT US

It's true. Our friends will mess up. They will not give us what we need. They will say strange, hurtful things that will confound us. They will drop the ball in all sorts of serious (and unserious) ways. Friends will let us down. But of course, we will also mess up. We will say the wrong thing or let someone down when they need us most. We may also say strange, hurtful things to others, even if our intentions are good.

The key to modern friendships is to take a step back and understand what we can control and what we can't. There's no such thing as a perfect friendship because there's no such thing as a perfect person. If we expect perfect friendships all the time from everyone we know, we will constantly have our hearts broken.

Like all living things, long friendships carry scars in the form of hurt feelings, misunderstandings, and conflicts. Your path with your friends won't be perfect. It may be rough, but that's okay. What matters is that we choose to invest our time and attention wisely and accept one another for how capable we are today.

TRUTH #2: FRIENDSHIPS WILL CHANGE

Friendships are not static, like a stop sign or a print issue of *Vogue* magazine. Instead, they are dynamic, like a tomato plant or Philadelphia's weather. People grow, change, and transform all the time, for many reasons. Therefore, our friendships also must grow, change, and transform.

Friendships, like TV shows and bears, have seasons of activity. Some seasons you'll be close and giddy. Other times, you might be cooler and separate. You will constantly be surprised in finding that friendships you considered dead and buried turn out to have more life in them. Some friendships are like *Cobra Kai*, rebooting after twenty-something years and becoming a hit once again. Whenever you feel certain about a friendship one way or another, life finds a way to surprise you.

Leanne's Experience

Sometimes friendships change in ways we won't be stoked about.

"I'm struggling to find friends who like to do the things I do," Leanne told me. "Most have moved (two to Paris, which is fun to visit but so, so far), so I'm left with the friends who only want to drink and go out when I want to be home, the friends with kids who have exactly one hour free every other Wednesday, and the ones who complain about money so much that either they won't go to the place I want to or I have to pay for them."

She continued, "I do wish someone told me that it was completely normal to lose friends at any age of life. I was under the impression that as an adult, everyone would just get along." What surprised her the most, though, was how many "close" friends abruptly stopped talking to her when her dad died. "It was extremely confusing, and over four years later, I still don't have answers," she said. "I guess I thought as an adult, if a friendship ended, there would be some clear closure."

In reality, closure isn't guaranteed. It's our responsibility to make peace with the ambiguity. One way to do that is to share your story with others. Process your hurt with the help of a mental health professional if you find yourself struggling to make sense of things. I'm also hopeful that reading a book like this could provide clues as to what might have happened with your friend. As we discuss why humans choose the behaviors they do, you might evaluate disappointments in a whole new light.

TRUTH #3: FRIENDSHIPS REQUIRE MATURITY

Friendship requires knowing yourself, knowing your emotional limits, and being explicit with others about your needs and wants. It takes maturity to understand yourself, to understand that the world is large, unpredictable, and complicated, and to communicate clearly about your limits instead of flaking on plans or blowing off milestone events. Regardless, it's important that you continue to reach out to your friends and make time for them.

None of us are born friendship experts. We're all a work in progress. But it's worth your time and attention to become a true, wholehearted friend to other people. When you look back at your life, when you think of how you spent your time, you will not regret the time you spend with people who make your life richer. And you will feel the satisfaction of bearing witness to your friends' struggles and triumphs.

It's okay if your friendships are floundering right now. You're up against historically new forces that we, as a culture, have very little experience navigating. And no two friendships are alike. Each brings its own magic, language, ceremony, and chemistry.

Just as the goal with meditation is to find peace and acceptance with the present moment rather than "find happiness," it's wiser, more realistic, and more mature to approach your friendships with the goal of accepting people and friendships as they are instead of trying to force closeness or resolution. People don't like being dominated, so efforts to coerce someone into a friendship will likely backfire. Letting go might be a new muscle for you, but keep practicing it, and it will get easier. Celebrate your failures because failure is evidence of trying!

Nowadays, it takes so little effort to attain the things I want. I can have squiggly hair elastics delivered to my house, I can watch episodes of *Veep* on demand, and I can order Rare Beauty Soft Pinch Liquid Blush online. Friendship is the opposite of that. It requires deliberate action and nuanced thought. High-quality friendships require us to expend our finite resources of time, energy, attention, and money. It's grueling precisely because it requires you to put skin in the game.

Sometimes friendships flounder due to simple logistics. Perhaps you struggle with finding a location to practice your friendship in a "third place"—apart from your workplace or home—in a time when there are fewer and fewer places to congregate for free. Our grandparents had clubs, organizations, and houses of worship, which made congregating easier, but if you don't have these low-lift places to meet, that's another factor you need to spend energy figuring out.

Of course, the flip side of effort is failure. When you try anything, you also run the risk of messing it up. I mess up constantly. I'm a walking encyclopedia of epic mess ups. Hell, I titled my humor memoir *Clearly, I Didn't Think This Through* BECAUSE I'm a walking fuckup. I've had quite a few friendship fallouts, some of which are still painful to think about all these years later. I've had best friends stop returning my phone calls. To this day, I still don't know why. I've said the wrong thing to my friends more times than I can count. I've let my friends down in all sorts of ways, big and small. I've sidestepped necessary, difficult conversations out of fear. I've let resentments fester until they've ballooned into unhealable wounds. I didn't know what I was doing.

So many of these hiccups could have been resolved if my friends and I had possessed the courage and maturity to broach these sticky issues. I saw conflict as a death sentence for a friendship, not a respectful negotiation that would lead to improved cohesion. It took losing these valuable friendships for me to understand that I had a lot of growing up to do. I knew I had attained maturity when I stopped pointing the finger at my friends so much and took accountability for the roles I played in these breakups. Maturity is the threshold you cross when you stop being defensive and start becoming curious: Why does my friend feel the way they feel? What part am I playing in this reaction? Having these conversations with an open heart and a calm mind let me know that I was finally mature enough to enjoy the deep friendships I craved.

There's something beautiful about messing up. Slipups, miscalculations, and gaffes are going to happen anytime you start making changes. It's part of the privilege of being alive. Animals mess up. I know bears mess up. Dogs definitely mess up. I'm sure there's a squid out there doing some gnarly, misguided shit right now. What matters is how we embrace our (normal, inevitable) fuckups.

Failure is important. It's an essential part of learning limits, boundaries, and preferences. My tattered trail of busted friendships is riddled with valuable lessons. Heck, I fought for those lessons. I'm a better friend because I've botched the assignment so many times.

In the end, these relationships are what define us. Your legacy is how you make the people close to you feel.

TRUTH #4: YOU NEED TO BE OKAY
WITH OCCASIONAL REJECTION

There's a good chance that you will be turned down, bailed on, or snubbed when you ask someone to spend time with you. It may be tempting to stop reaching out for fear of it happening again, but it is your responsibility to keep trying to maintain the friendship (within reason, of course).

Meaningful friendships will always come with some level of rejection. No friend will be available 100 percent of the time. Sure, you might get spurned, ignored, or slighted at points; and it will hurt to feel rebuffed, to hear a no when you request help or organize a hangout. A lack of a response or a no is not always cause for concern, but it is useful information about how your friend prioritizes the relationship.

Lainey's Experience

"I wish I would have known that not everyone wants engagement all of the time," Lainey told me. "Some friends are okay to see each other once a quarter or once a year, and that doesn't mean our friendship is any less meaningful."

Maxine's Experience

"Some of my friendships have crumbled for one reason or another: they moved, they had a kid, or we simply just stopped texting each other," Maxine said. "For most, there are no hard or awkward feelings or anything; we just don't really keep in touch. For a few others, I allowed our lax communication during the pandemic to let the friendship fizzle, as it felt like it had already run its course."

I wish I could wave a wand and take the possibility of rejection or neglect away, but that is what makes friendships a marvel. Diamonds are valuable because they're perceived to be rare. (Even though they actually aren't. I know, I know, just Google it.) Caviar is expensive because it's difficult to cultivate. And have you ever seen one of those intense crabbing shows that show fishermen in Alaska wrangling jangly nets in intense sea storms? That's why Alaskan king crab legs are so dang pricey!

The rarity of the thing usually makes it feel special, and friendships are no different. The possibility of risking emotional rejection, and each person's commitment to intentionally avoid it, is what makes friendships special.

In his book *The Four Agreements*, Don Miguel Ruiz outlines four rules for living a great life. His first rule is to be impeccable with your word, and his second rule is to not take anything personally. "Personal importance, or taking things personally, is the maximum expression of selfishness because we make the assumption that everything is about 'me,'" he wrote. "Nothing other people do is because of you. It is because of themselves. All people live in their own dream, in their own mind; they are in a completely different world from the one we live in. When we take something personally, we make the assumption that they know what is in our world and we try to impose our world on their world . . . then you feel offended and your reaction is to defend your beliefs and create conflicts."[1]

Ruiz takes this idea even further, almost to an extreme. "When we really see other people as they are without taking it personally, we can never be hurt by what they say or do. Even if others lie to you, it's okay. They are lying to you because they are afraid. They are afraid you will discover that they are not perfect."

By letting go of the need to control others, Ruiz tells us that we will find we don't need to trust other people as much as we need to trust ourselves to make the right choices. Anger, jealousy, sadness—all of it will lessen when you decide not to take things so personally and feel hurt, neglected, offended, or betrayed at someone else's actions because, at the end of the day, they most likely are not trying to intentionally hurt you.

Olivia's Experience

Olivia knows it's smart to keep her ego in check when it comes to her friendships. When sharing a story with her therapist about a friend who slighted her, the therapist challenged her: "What if your friend just had a blind spot? You don't have to do anything to address the blind spot. Just move on." That reframe liberated her. "She had a blind spot. She wasn't intentionally trying to do something that hurt me. She's got her own stuff going on. And it freed me up to forgive, to not take it to heart so much," Olivia said.

And that's really the bottom line here: Friends are people. People have blind spots. Therefore, by the transitive property of blind spots, friends have blind spots too! Of course, people sometimes do have bad intentions. It's an unfortunate reality that sometimes friends do treat us badly on purpose, which can trigger a crisis in the friendship. More on how to handle that in chapter 9.

TRUTH #5: IT'S ON US TO LOOK FOR OPPORTUNITIES FOR CONNECTION

Popping into T.J. Maxx is a spiritual experience for me. I love everything about the store: the harsh overhead fluorescent lighting, the rows of shelves lined with hand soaps and 64-ounce bottles of lotion, the whimsical seasonal mug displays. This location in South Philly had Easter-themed pillows out on display at the end of January, but that's the way T.J. Maxx rolls! It doesn't wait for you to be emotionally ready for a new holiday season. It sets its own calendar, baby. T.J. Maxx bows down to no one.

One day, as I was scanning the hair product section, I noticed there were two JVN conditioners, made by *Queer Eye*'s Jonathan van Ness, on the shelf. The bottle was marked $12.99, which isn't bad for a full-size bottle of a name-brand conditioner that typically retails for $21 at Sephora. We can all agree that was a good-ish deal.

A tall blonde lady noticed me eyeing the bottle of conditioner, so she picked up the glossy blue bottle, turned to me, and said, "This conditioner is the bomb."

"Yeah, I've heard good things about the brand," I replied.

"Dude, it's all true," she said. "You should definitely get one. Believe me, you won't regret it."

I picked up the bottle, and, wordlessly, we toasted each other with our conditioner bottles, tapping them together and nodding. Two strangers, two T.J. Maxx shoppers at 1:30 pm on a Thursday, two people enjoying a small electric moment of spontaneous conditioner-focused friendship.

The magic moment was created because I took the woman's bid to try the conditioner. Friends love it when you take their bid ("listen to this podcast," "watch this TV show") because you are telling them, "I value your opinion. I'm open to seeing the world through your eyes." I honestly didn't even need conditioner at that time, but I was so tickled at the quick camaraderie we developed that I just went with it.

In marriage therapist John Gottman's book *The Relationship Cure: A 5 Step Guide to Strengthening Your Marriage, Family, and Friendships*, he noted that successful couples are more attentive to one another, and he defined our friendly bids with one another as a fundamental unit of emotional connection.[2] Taking bids offers evidence that we care about one another.

Taking or ignoring a bid is an answer to someone's request for emotional connection. "A bid can be a question, a gesture, a look, a touch—any single expression that says, 'I want to feel connected to you,'" he wrote. In his initial research, Gottman focused on romantic relationships but soon saw an overlap in all relationships we have.

He found that, couples who engaged in each other's bids enjoyed higher rates of positive engagement, which allowed for greater access to expressions of humor, affection, and interest in arguments. "It's almost as if all the good feelings they've accumulated by responding respectfully and lovingly to one another's bids form a pot of emotional 'money in the bank,'" he wrote.

For those who take less of these bids in their relationships, they're rarely motivated by malice. According to Gottman, it's much more common to neglect a bid out of ignorance or insensitivity. Dismissing loved ones' bids creates a deep loneliness and disappointment. "Many describe peers, siblings, and children as disloyal, unworthy of trust," he added. However, once he dug deeper with these people, he saw a recognizable pattern: his clients seemed totally unaware of the bids for connection that people in their life made toward them. It was no wonder that people stopped initiating bids if their efforts were being blown off.

Bids, Gottman explains, can be big like a marriage proposal or small like refilling their glass of water. They can be subtle: "I like you in blue. It's your color." Or explicit: "Can you give me a haircut?" Bids can happen between strangers: "Can you watch my laptop while I run to the restroom?" And of course they can happen between best friends: "I heard this new podcast I think you'll like."

Positive responses could sound something like, "Oooh, send me the link to the episode. I'll listen on my commute home," which shows you're receptive to the bid and potentially leads to continued interaction. Later on, you can continue the conversation with your friend by sharing your impressions of the podcast and possibly building a common interest.

Negative responses could sound like, "I don't listen to podcasts; they're not my thing." This kind of response prunes the branch of connection, so to speak. The chances that your friend will attempt to offer a subsequent bid is closer to zero. Of course Gottman doesn't recommend saying yes to every invitation that slides into your inbox. That's not realistic nor is that sustainable. Instead, he recommends when refusing the invitation being careful to accept the bid for emotional connection. So if someone recommends a podcast and you're not a fan of podcasts, it's better to say, "I don't listen to podcasts; they're not my thing. I do like reading newsletters, though. Do you subscribe to any that you love?"

In this example, you turn down the bid but offer an additional positive response that will assure the other person that you're still open to connection. Taking small bids when they arise is a brilliant strategy to maintaining ties.

TRUTH #6: BEING SOMEONE'S BEST FRIEND WILL MAKE *YOU* FEEL HAPPIER

When it comes to friendship, I think most people imagine they'd be happier with a robust web of engaged friends. A 2019 study by researchers Suzanne Degges-White, a professor at Northern Illinois University and the author of *Toxic Friendships: Knowing the Rules and Dealing with the Friends Who Break Them*, and Marcela Kepic interviewed 422 women between the ages of 31 and 77 and examined how their friendships influence their life satisfaction.[3] They found that there were three main factors that were predictive of life satisfaction in midlife women: (1) feeling younger than your chronological age, (2) enjoying a sense of belonging, and (3) being someone's best friend. Highlight this shit! This is a road map to contentment, y'all.

They also found that having more frequent visits with friends, feeling satisfied with the number of one's friends, and having a larger number of friends in general all imparted a higher level of life satisfaction. It makes perfect sense that having more friends in our network makes us happier.

Numbers-wise, the study found that having three or more good friends was indicative of higher levels of life satisfaction.

However, you may be surprised to learn why it's pleasurable to have a set of valued friends. Sure, it feels good to have someone to call and give us emotional support. But, as it turns out, being considered someone's best friend really homed in on where the wonderful feelings emerge.

"Having a best friend doesn't contribute to life satisfaction, but being someone's best friend does," Dr. Degges-White said. "Because a lot of times we think, 'Well, I've got a best friend, so I'm good.' But it's really 'Does someone consider me their best friend?' Someone considering you a best friend is a good measure of how giving and supportive you are, and it's more likely to predict life satisfaction rather than saying, 'I've got best friends I can count on,'" she said.

Why does it feel so good to be someone's best friend? Because we're biologically wired for it. Altruism—being concerned with other people's welfare—is an evolutionary survival tool we developed in order to keep society chugging along. We're hardwired to want to help others.[4]

"When we do something nice for someone else, we get a hit of dopamine, and we get the good feels," Dr. Degges-White said. "Being a good friend is going to feed us and nurture us and give us that positive reward. It's not just so much having friends you can lean on, but *being* the friend that someone else can lean on that really feels good to us and makes us feel like we matter to other people."

We all want to matter to the people in our lives. The way to do that is to support and care for them.

Love and belonging are just some of our basic genetic needs. It's crucial that we feel like we're part of something bigger than ourselves. Friendships do that for us. Friends check in on us when we feel upset or disappointed, and they make us feel important to them, which gives our self-esteem an incredible boost.

Going back to the three main factors for life satisfaction in middle-aged women, Drs. Degges-White and Kepic found that one typically feels younger than their chronological age when they are active in their community.[5] According to them, this community engagement helps folks feel young at heart, find joy and pleasure in life, go with the flow, and engage in new activities. Along those same lines, to enjoy a sense of belonging, you have to create and nurture the communities you're in. You need to practice diligence by showing up and putting effort into keeping your friendships alive.

And how to be someone's best friend? Well, this book is literally a manual on how to do just that. Keep reading.

To recap, having friends we admire and love is great, but having wonderful, dynamic people consider us *their* best friend is an even *more* incredible feeling. That's because we love feeling needed and that we belong. It makes us feel like we matter to others. THIS is the antidote to loneliness.

WELCOME TO WHOLEHEARTED FRIENDSHIP

After almost a decade of research and countless conversations, I've finally arrived at a place where I understand what it takes to be seen as the dedicated, caring friend that you are. I call this body of decisions **Wholehearted Friendship**.

Researcher and author Brené Brown uses the word *wholehearted* a lot in her work. She speaks about wholehearted living, which she describes as engaging in our lives from a place of worthiness. And she talks about cultivating the courage and compassion "to wake up in the morning and think, 'No matter what gets done and how much is left undone, I am enough.'"

In my paradigm, I'm using the word *wholehearted* in a slightly different way. Wholehearted Friendship closes the gap between what you want your friendships to look like and how your friendships actually are. We achieve Wholehearted Friendship by paying attention to the things we think, say, and do—both to ourselves and our friends. This means being realistic about what you can achieve with the tools you have. It's about making wiser choices with the help of science to protect your high-quality friendships and give them the best chance to fit the different seasons of your life.

Why do friendships matter at all? If you've had a rocky track record with friends, you might wonder why you'd put yourself in a position to get hurt again. You might even convince yourself that friends aren't worth the hassle. They're too much trouble. Other people are complicated. They're a time sink. They come with their own problems and neuroses. Perhaps you prefer the company of animals or children. They seem safer. Less energy. Less work.

To that I'd say perhaps you haven't experienced the peaks of true Whole-hearted Friendship yet. I'm sorry you've had a rough road. But you're a wonderful, dimensional person who has a lot to offer the world, and it's time you find people who are a good fit for your life today.

We're never really taught how to be good friends to each other. As kids, perhaps it's assumed we'll learn this naturally through our interactions at school and in our neighborhoods. And whatever friendship-making hab-its we form in those early years, we carry with us into adulthood (with maybe some small adjustments here or there). As children, those limited skills might be passable because friendships are *waaaaaay* simpler. But as we mature into adults with complex lives, those interpersonal limitations become apparent; and they're often compounded by the pressures of our technology-driven, post-pandemic world. Until I reported on friendships, most of what I learned about being a friend was through trial and error. I don't want you to suffer the same mistakes I made.

The term *wholehearted* means to feel devoted, committed, and enthu-siastic, and Wholehearted Friendship is a perspective you adopt that embodies these traits. In this kind of relationship, you feel warm, comfort-able, and flexible, as if your favorite pair of leggings became sentient and sent you a funny meme from your favorite Will Ferrell movie.

Becoming a wholehearted friend changes the way you think and move through the world. It's about being selective with what you do, say, and think so those you care about feel confident, safe, and secure in your pres-ence. It's making yourself aware of other people's realities so they feel seen and heard. It's standing up for yourself and articulating what you need out of your relationships.

Isn't that how we all want to feel? Isn't that how *you* want to feel? Hope-fully you're nodding in agreement right now.

After doing the suggested exercises in this book, you'll quickly notice changes within yourself. You won't need to guess at how to respond to a friend in distress. You'll be more adept at identifying opportunities to deepen your bond. And you'll also apply what you've learned to other important people in your life, including your family members, significant other, colleagues, and acquaintances. Deepening these relationships and having a strong, healthy network of people you truly care about will help you face challenges no matter how steep they may be.

As you make these adjustments, the people in your life may notice positive changes in their relationships with you too. They'll notice that they seem calmer and more relaxed around you. They might feel safer opening up to you because they know they won't be judged for their feelings. They'll find themselves feeling validated, more understood, and better supported as they share the details of their lives. My hope is that this book will enable you to quickly diagnose why your friendships are suffering and what adjustments you can make to get them back on track so you can feel more empowered to let go of friendships you've outgrown, and feel more comfortable advocating for what you need and want in the friendships you decide to keep.

So how do we become indispensable to our friends? How do we get others to bring us close? How do we nail down the definition of "friends" beyond those we encounter on social media or at school or work? Well, the first step is to get real about who's truly in our network. Only then can we become a fantastic friend by changing, adapting, and orienting our lives in a way that allows our friendships space to grow.

3

Why You Feel Like You Have Both 100 Friends and Zero Friends

According to Georg Simmel, an influential early twentieth-century sociologist, most people's social network in premodern Western society was high in safety but low in tolerance for outsiders.[1] If you sketched out this social network, it would look like a series of concentric circles, with the innermost circle representing you, then moving out to your family unit, occupation, and broader community, with your religion and cultural identity comprising the outer circles.

Simmel found that societies that operate like this have some strengths. For one, folks feel more secure in close-knit communities, and there's also less ambiguity because people are raised knowing what's expected of them. They know their roles and cultural obligations, like who to marry or what occupations are acceptable. It takes a lot of guesswork out of the equation, so life is generally more linear.

My relatives living in a Romanian Jewish shtetl in the late 1800s lived like this within insulated Jewish communities. Women were limited to a few societal roles, and they certainly didn't attend college. Men probably worked in their family's business. And everyone in the community attended the same synagogue. There were strong *Fiddler on the Roof* vibes,

I'm sure. Your relatives probably lived in a community like this too back in the day.

The drawback of societies like this, however, is that individual freedom is seen as a weakness, and as a result, anything outside of the group is considered suspicious and is rarely tolerated.

Even though I've used the term *premodern* to describe this kind of society, it still exists today, more commonly in the form of cults or other highly rigid communities where outsiders are discouraged from participating.

In modern society, though, our social network is visualized as a smattering of intersecting circles—some chosen, some inherited. You don't get to choose your family of origin, but it isn't as necessary to stay near them for your entire life as it may have been one hundred years ago. As a result, modern society's network is high on information and choice rather than kinship and place, potentially looking more like a complex Venn diagram than a series of concentric circles, with each aspect of life and community overlapping, but not overtaking, another.

While we don't have as strong of a societal bedrock, we do have more individual choice over factors like which jobs we take and which schools we attend (if at all), we're more tolerant of outsiders, and we're more open to exploring different parts of our lives. The downside is that this kind of society has more uncertainty. It gets harder to answer a question like "Who are you?" because the answer may not be so simple. You might feel a pull on your values and norms depending on the groups you choose to identify with, like your race, nationality, class, political associations, job, or even residence. There are a lot of identities to juggle!

According to Bernice Pescosolido and Beth Rubin in their 2000 published study in the *American Sociological Review*, we are in an "era of societal transition."[2] We now exist in a postmodern society that resembles a spoke (think: a bicycle wheel), with you in the middle and every other aspect of your identity branching off on its own.

In this postmodern social network, there are no overlapping social circles because we typically don't stay in a group long enough to solidify strong ties. Instead, individuals' connections to institutions "are multiple and often temporary, not single and lifelong," the authors wrote. "Individuals have connections to many workplaces, to many families, perhaps even to more than one religion."[3]

If premodern society is a tree with deep roots, postmodern society is a butterfly; rather than planting roots in one spot, we flutter around. This spoke structure also reflects the economic reality for most of us; we often don't work the same job for forty years anymore like our parents and grandparents did. We move around often, spending a few years here, a few years there, and we tend to take on more short-term projects with a variety of employers. Our relationships—social, intimate, and religious—now thrive on flexibility rather than stability. As Pescosolido and Rubin said, "Freedom and choice exist on an unprecedented scale."[4] More importantly, you can drop a set of social ties and have other sources of adequate support. You may not speak with your group of friends from college anymore, but you have a new group of friends in your town, so it's all good.

What's interesting about this social setup is that there is so much more pressure on the individual to keep up connection. Pescosolido and Rubin said postmodern society "requires constant negotiation between husbands and wives, between employees and employers, between clergy and their congregations." Um, this sounds stressful. They also said, "Social relationships can neither be taken for granted nor can they survive for long without attention, particularly under situations that stress the bonds themselves or individuals' ability to maintain these bonds. There is a certain fragility to social relations because they are not supported by webs of relationship that crisscross social life."[5]

You guys, I feel *so seen* by these findings. It's not in your head if you've been feeling the stress of holding up your entire social network because that's exactly what's most likely happening. Yes, we are the center of this spoke model. Yes, we have unprecedented choice and flexibility in who we associate with. But we also bear the entire weight of propping up our individual networks that often don't overlap. That means there's no one to share the burden of making plans or finding reasons to get together. In a spoke model, the reasons a friendship should persist have to come from *us*. We have to make the case to each other that our friendship should continue. There's no magical entity or closed community supergluing our friendships in place. We have to create meaning for them, and we have to do the hard work of renewing connection.

My writer friends in Philly do not know my college friends in New York City, just as my college friends don't know my high school friends in Chicago. They're all separate, autonomous city-states, not a cohesive union. The fluidity of our friendships and the transient nature of these ties exists *because* we live a society that's also fluid and transient. Of course our relationships are bound to reflect that. Living in this spoke model system creates a unique pain that is different from earlier generations.

"Freedom of choice in social life increases the potential for alienation, isolation, and fragmentation. The potential to 'fall through the cracks' is enormous," Pescosolido and Rubin wrote.[6] That's what it feels like when your community is splintered or, worse, nonexistent.

Jeannie's Experience

Jeannie feels like she has both over a hundred friends and absolutely no friends. "Some days I feel strongly connected to a network of people. I feel seen, heard, understood, and enjoyed by others. Other days I feel totally alone, completely overlooked, and frustrated with my lack of day-to-day friends that live right near me."

She has good friends from many different phases of her life: camp, high school, college, grad school, neighbors. But these groups all live in different places, and they don't overlap. She's jealous of her friends who have local networks with female friends, couple friends, family friends, and everything in between.

"I don't feel like I have that variety anywhere," she said. She's stumped at who'd she'd even ask to get together with on a regular Friday night. She doesn't have close, long-term relationships with people who are within a five-mile radius of her house.

"And that makes a really big difference. Because when I look out and I see people who have these very close ties with people in our neighborhood or through school, that makes me feel so jealous." She has to remind herself that she has friends too; they're just . . . not close by.

"I know that I do have these important relationships, but they're not next to me," she said. "That is really hard." She's always on the hunt for new friends, but she doesn't have the bandwidth to nourish new friendships.

"I *want* to have plans to go out to dinner. I want to go to a concert and have someone to go with me, all those things," she said. "How do I manage that out of the people who I know are dedicated to me forever and have no ability to see me regularly versus the people who like would be able to see me all the time? But I don't necessarily know that we have what it takes to be even medium short-term friends. It still takes a lot of work and effort."

"JUST MAKE SOME NEW FRIENDS," PEOPLE SAY.

If you're wondering where potential friends are, they're literally all around you. According to The Survey Center on American Life published in May 2021,[7] people tend to make close friends:

- At work
- At school
- Through an existing network of friends
- Through a close friend in their neighborhood
- At their place of worship
- At a club or organization they belong to
- Through their child's school
- Online

Sometimes we keep friends around simply because we've already invested so much time in the relationship. In fact, the survey asked respondents what made someone their best friend, and the most common answer was longevity. By default, we typically designate someone as our best friend based on how long we've known them and who's been by our side through life's ups and downs.

Of course, there is value in having friends who have known so many versions of you. They know your background, your family members, your challenges, your triumphs. Remember that stat about how long it takes to make a close friend? Over two hundred hours of shared activities. So, yeah, investing time is super important. But you may find that just because you've had a friend for a long time doesn't mean you're a perfect fit forever.

Dartmouth Sociologist Janice McCabe analyzed the personal friendship networks of sixty-seven U.S. college students in the Midwest and found that the students, of varying race and class, coalesced into three distinctive types: tight-knitters, compartmentalizers, and samplers. Each group has their own liberties and pressures.[8]

Tight-knitters have one densely woven friendship group in which nearly all their friends are friends with one another. In this way, this type of personal network resembles a ball of yarn. She found this group to consist of mostly Black and Latina/o students, as they found refuge with each other on a predominately White campus.

- Pros: Tremendously strong social support. Members of this group consider others as family and reported that they feel at home with them. This "yarn" group of tight-knitters had the power to lift each other up, whether academically or socially. For example, if the majority of the group members valued academic achievement, that attitude would become infectious for everyone else.

- Cons: The opposite was also true. If the majority of the friends weren't engaged in school work, others in the group were at a greater risk of being negatively influenced. In this case, the group felt their friends were a "constant" distraction from their studies.

Compartmentalizers make friends in clusters of two to four, where friends know each other within clusters but rarely across them. This could look like having a group of friends from home to watch movies and go out with and a group of friends at school to study with. This network resembles a bow tie (cute!). Most of the White students in the study fell into this group, although there were some exceptions. This group received average social and academic support from these different clusters.

- Pros: Students could easily oscillate between the "fun" group of friends and the "support" group of friends. Wendy, a Black compartmentalizer identified in the study, found a support system within a cluster of Black friends in her academic major, and she identified this group as being instrumental in her social success at college.

- Cons: The study found that students with more than two clusters of friends felt a dual sense of pressure on their time and identity to keep up with multiple friendship groups. Yes, the clusters provided a sense of belonging, which felt great, but maintaining social ties with different groups was often demanding, "and these demands escalated with each additional cluster."

Samplers make a friend or two from a variety of places, but the friends remain unconnected to each other. This personal network resembles a daisy. This group had the biggest range of class and race backgrounds, but it was also the most disconnected. Steve, profiled in the study, reported meeting one person at a specific place, club, or event, then rinse and repeat. Yes, he had a robust number of friends, but he didn't feel any particular sense of social support. Instead, he felt isolated.

- Pros: Samplers usually were self-motivated and exceeded academically without relying heavily on their friends. To them, friends were the fun people who didn't influence them too heavily.

- Cons: This group is the most independent group but also the most precarious. This was the only group to describe their friendships as feeling disappointing. McCabe found that this group reported feeling the loneliest and the most lacking in social support. This makes sense because there's little cohesion in their friend group. They lacked "the breadth and depth provided by tight-knitters' full network and the adequate support provided by compartmentalizers' clusters." So it's basically the worst of both worlds.

"Tight-knitters benefit from social support, but need to watch out for friends who can distract them or drag them down academically," McCabe wrote. "Compartmentalizers find balance in social and academic involvement from different clusters, and samplers appear academically successful but often feel socially isolated."[9]

Granted, this is a small sample size to draw conclusions from, but the idea of different personal social networks can help us understand why we feel the way we do about our friend groups.

Those with daisy networks tend to be the ones having the most trouble with this whole modern friendship thing because like Jeannie, they have friends; they just don't live nearby or know anyone else in their other circles.

Even though these results focused on college-age adults, it's worth thinking about how these results translate to postcollege life. When McCabe interviewed the subjects five years later, she found less variation in young adults' postcollege networks compared to college. But she did find some remaining differences across network types. For instance, "compartmentalizers remained compartmentalizers, and tight-knitters generally stayed tight-knitters, but the samplers mostly became tight-knitters too."[10]

In adulthood, we can slip into the same patterns. If you're active in a religious community, it's likely that all or a good portion of your close friends attend the same church or synagogue (tight-knitter/yarn). You might rock a bow tie with your work friends in one silo and your competitive dancing friends or whatever in another (compartmentalizer/bow tie). Or, you might hang out with a variety of friends from different parts of your life who never meet each other (sampler/daisy).

One thing friendship expert Dr. Jeffrey A. Hall wants you to know is that if your social network is fractured, your loneliness is not your fault. A University of Kansas Professor of Communication Studies, Dr. Hall is sensitive to the fact that giving people advice about trying to build and grow their friendships contributes to the expectation that people take care of problems that are beyond them. He doesn't want to blame people who are lonely or without friends for their own situation.

"I'm not trying to make people the bad person for what they're struggling with. Because the truth is, the conditions that we're living in is a struggle for everybody. Some people are going to struggle more than others," Dr. Hall told me.[11] "It's important for us to be sympathetic and kind to the fact that many folks are in the situation that they don't want to be in under no failings of their own. They didn't do anything wrong. That's just the world we live in."

Understanding these sociological forces is the first step to empowerment. If society doesn't hand us the kind of community we're yearning for, we need to create it for ourselves. That's what being a part of the punk scene in high school taught me. We were the freaks and outcasts of our communities, so we banded together and created something awesome. You can too! Anyone can. If you're in a daisy network and feel like your needs aren't being met, maybe you'll be motivated to create more of a yarn or bow-tie network for yourself. There's always hope as long as the desire is present.

Exercise: Identify Your IRL Social Network

Are you a tight-knitter in a yarn ball, a compartmentalizer in a bow tie, or a sampler in a daisy?

Choose one: While growing up, your social network was generally: yarn / bow tie / daisy.

How did you feel having a social network in that shape?

Pros: _____

_____

_____

Cons:_____

_____

_____

Choose one: While in high school, your social network was generally: yarn / bow tie / daisy.

How did you feel having a social network in that shape?

Pros: _____

_____

_____

Cons:_____

_____

_____

Choose one: While in college, your social network was generally: yarn / bow tie / daisy.

How did you feel having a social network in that shape?

Pros: _____

_____

_____

Cons:_____

_____

_____

Choose one: Postcollege, your social network was generally: yarn / bow tie / daisy.

How did you feel having a social network in that shape?

Pros: _____

_____

_____

Cons:_____

_____

_____

Choose one: In your twenties, your social network was generally:
yarn / bow tie / daisy.

How did you feel having a social network in that shape?

Pros: _____

_____

_____

Cons:_____

_____

_____

Choose one: In your thirties, your social network was generally:
yarn / bow tie / daisy.

How did you feel having a social network in that shape?

Pros: _____

_____

_____

Cons:_____

_____

_____

Choose one: In your forties and beyond, your social network was generally: yarn / bow tie / daisy.

How did you feel having a social network in that shape?

Pros: _____

_____

_____

Cons:_____

_____

_____

In your journal of choice, reflect on which type of networks made you feel most supported and happiest. Which made you feel least supported and lonelier? Taking time to consider the personal networks you've been in throughout your life will help you pinpoint what works best for you and perhaps where your social struggles occur most. For example, maybe you'll understand why you struggled so hard in college if you had more of a daisy network going on but you thrive in a bow-tie situation.

My hope is that by seeing the variety of personal networks you've had, you'll get some new information about yourself along with a new language to understand how these kinds of friendship networks operate. Maybe you loved being in a yarn network in your earlier years, so as you think about the kind of friend network you'll curate today, you might want to seek out a more yarn-like community. Maybe you'll realize that you found those yarn networks to be limiting and much prefer the flexibility of a bow-tie network.

In the next chapter, I'll explain how to find those like-minded people who will populate the community of your dreams. By understanding why we choose the friends we do, we can give ourselves the best chance of having meaningful and nourishing connections.

4

Why We Crave Friendships Even Though People Are Baffling

Friendships, by design, are confusing because human beings are confusing. As a species, I have to say that we're not always predictable or logical. We know we should exercise, but we lie on the couch all day. We know we should cut sugar out of our diet, but we can't stop nibbling on the Thin Mints in our freezer (which is the best way to eat them, in my humble opinion). That's the human condition.

Also, like a healthy lifestyle, friendships are the culmination of small, good decisions instead of one big, grand gesture (in much the same way that a single killer workout does not yield an immediate chiseled six-pack). Friendships require vigilance to make sure we're emotionally attuned to the other person and meeting their needs and expectations. And that our friends meet our needs and expectations too. That's a lot of needs and expectations flying around that often go unspoken.

In addition to our previously mentioned tendency to not always make the healthiest decisions, we are in a historically confusing time for friendship. We love our friends even though we don't always love the effort of keeping in touch with them. Even if you feel some negative feelings toward expending energy on your besties, you are NOT a crappy friend. It's never been cheaper or easier to drop a line to a friend, but paradoxically, because it takes so little effort to fire off a text message or voice memo, the gesture often doesn't feel special or meaningful. It's an appetizer of communication instead of a hearty main course.

The buffet of modes of communication are overwhelming. Should you text or call, send an email or DM, FaceTime or leave a voice memo? It's maddening. I get flustered trying to guess when's a good time to reach out. Is it better to text in the morning or call in the afternoon? Should I send a courier pigeon at the stroke of midnight or wait for them to contact me via smoke signal? I'm afraid of seeming needy or annoying or exposing myself to disappointment if my friend never responds. There can be a lot of anxiety around something that *should* feel easy.

The first rule of friendships is to drop the word *should* altogether, as it's not a useful word. In general, it sets us up for disappointment and causes us to focus on how things would be ideally, not how they actually are.

HOW CHOICE THEORY CAN HELP US UNDERSTAND WHY WE HAVE THE FRIENDS WE DO

In his book *Choice Theory: A New Psychology of Personal Freedom*, psychiatrist William Glasser said all behavior is purposeful. "All we can do from birth to death is behave," he wrote.[1] All behavior—otherwise known as our total behavior—is made up of four inseparable components: acting (walking, talking, eating, etc.), thinking (evaluating), feeling (pain, pleasure), and physiology (heart pumping, lungs breathing, neurochemistry neurochemistry-ing). These four components occur simultaneously and are inseparable. They are what it means to be a living, breathing, thinking human.

Regardless of these often automatic bodily responses, there are two things to know: (1) you can control your actions and thoughts, and (2) we always try to make the best choice at any given time, but the best choice doesn't mean it's necessarily healthy or good. This concept of choice is what Dr. Glasser calls **Choice Theory**.

We do all things—avoid opening a letter from the IRS, doom-scroll through our phones before bedtime, wonder about how an ex is doing—for an innate and limited set of reasons, which Glasser calls **Basic Human Needs:**[2]

- **Physical survival** is about feeling safe and secure through sustaining your life, including maintaining your overall health, securing shelter, and attaining nourishment.

- **Love and belonging** explains our desire to be connected with friends, family, romantic partners, coworkers, pets, and other groups. Psychologically, this need involves feeling loved and valued.

- **Power** speaks to our need to hold influence, achieve goals, and have a healthy sense of self-worth. We want to matter, be competent and respected, and have our efforts make a difference in the world. This need includes boosting our self-esteem and speaks to our desire to leave a lasting legacy.

- **Freedom** is about exercising independence and moving freely in the world without restriction. Creativity and self-expression are also included here. This need is about feeling autonomous.

- **Fun** is about playing, seeking out pleasures, relaxing, and learning.

These needs are universal, which means we all have them. Yes, even the person who delivers your mail and the lady who shade-matched your foundation at Sephora. These five needs are woven into the human experience and can overlap, change from minute to minute, or conflict with the needs of other people. For example, my need to have fun at work might clash with my boss's need to maintain a professional relationship with her employees.

Everything we do is our best attempt to get what we want with the information and skills available to us in the moment. It's important to note that while these basic needs can be delayed, they cannot be denied completely, and only we can decide when our needs are truly satisfied.

While all humans have these five basic needs, how we go about attaining them differs from person to person. The second part of choice theory says we all have a personal picture album of the people, things, ideas, and ideals that we think will increase the quality of our lives. This picture album is called our **Quality World**. Our individual motivations—why we love one person over another, why we pursue one career over another—are ultimately in service of making our Quality World as close to our reality as possible.

For instance, at a basic level, you need love and belonging, but you're not likely to marry any person you cross paths with to fulfill this need. Instead, you're more likely to select a specific person to marry who has the best chance to fulfill that need for the long term. Similarly, if you're hungry, you won't nibble on just anything in your sight line. Instead, you'll select a particular food—a crisp apple, a comforting sleeve of Oreos—to get you closer to your ideal world.

Modern life is a Cheesecake Factory menu with an endless array of options. (Seriously, have you seen those massive menus? They're like an employee training manual.) When faced with an overwhelming number of choices at a chain restaurant, we must decide what to order. Our mood, our appetite, our food preferences, our finances, and more all influence what we ultimately decide on. One person orders roasted salmon because it's heart healthy. Another person orders lemon raspberry cheesecake because it's their birthday. Same restaurant, different highly personal reasons for ordering their food, but at the root of it is the same desire to make their Quality World a reality.

My theory is that Glasser's Choice Theory framework applies to our web of friendships as well. You may be pulling some friends close and distancing yourself from others based on which basic needs are most important to you at any given time. When you're hungry, that survival need comes to the forefront, so you stop what you're doing and grab lunch. And when you're lonely, you'll feel compelled to call a friend instead of watch TV. Here are other ways Choice Theory might influence the decisions you make:

- **Survival.** Ideally, people work to have some security in their lives. You keep friends close who help you out in a practical way. Perhaps they can take you to a doctor's visit or babysit your kids, for instance. When you're stressed, and a friend isn't stepping up to take some of the burden off your shoulders, you might downgrade their importance in your life.

- **Love and belonging.** Friends who make you feel loved and included in their lives address this need. So you might distance yourself from those who criticize or alienate you. Belonging helps you feel like you and your feelings matter, that you're cared about and cared for.

- **Power.** Professional opportunities are often determined by who you know, which is why networking is so crucial to establishing a successful career. Maybe you keep certain friends close based on their ability to introduce you to other powerful people or help you with professional opportunities. Or, on the flip side of this, perhaps you have a dynamic in your friendships where your friend always gives you unsolicited advice as a way to maintain a level of personal power over you.

- **Freedom.** This need speaks to our innate desire to express ourselves and be creative. Perhaps you distance yourself from friends who judge you or with whom you feel you have to behave a certain way that doesn't align with your sense of independence. If you've ever thought, *I can really be myself around this person,* then they help you feel free. Freedom could look like dying your hair pink, attending a Pride parade, or chasing big dreams. Freedom is how art is made, songs are sung, paintings are painted, and words are written.

- **Fun.** I mean, what's better than having fun with a buddy? Obviously, you realize sometimes friendships aren't exactly a barrel of monkeys. They can be exhausting or full of friction. That may be why you put certain friendships aside. The thoughtless friend who dominates your time together with rants about their no-good significant other, the friend who always seems to have one crisis after another, the self-absorbed friend who can't muster interest in your professional accomplishments—none of these people feel great to be around. If the fun factor is low, you may find yourself distancing yourself from that friend.

WHY PEOPLE MAKE FRIENDS

Glasser's basic needs of survival, love and belonging, power, freedom, and fun dovetail with what Apostolou and Keramari found in their 2020 paper that studied the reasons why people make friends in the first place.[3] Those reasons include:

- **Social assistance and advice:** having people around to support and advise them
- **Mating:** securing a romantic partner
- **Career:** having better cooperation in their work environment and help in advancing their professional development
- **Desirable traits:** being around people with positive traits such as trustworthiness and integrity
- **Socializing:** communicating with other people in order to avoid feeling lonely

Interestingly, these also relate to the genetic needs identified in choice theory. It's not a mystery why we pick the friends we do. Maybe you've never consciously considered why you picked your friends in the first place, but the reality is that there are all sorts of psychological reasons at play.

I'm just saying there's synergy here, people.

FRIENDSHIP BETWEEN GENDERS

All through my twenties, I had several close friendships with men who were like brothers to me. We'd stuck by each other's sides through typical twenties ups and downs like job changes, life stresses, and heartbreaks. But as we reached our early thirties, our solo hangouts dwindled, friendly texts went unanswered, and my upbeat emails ("Dude, I miss you! It's been too long. I miss your face. Let's hang!") were met with the digital equivalent of crickets. These friendships ended with a pitiful hiss, which was both confusing and painful. It never crossed my mind that these friendships would eventually tank, as we had maintained a closeness through so much turmoil in our twenties. In a Carrie Bradshaw-esque way, I couldn't help but wonder what was it about *now* that made these guy friends bail?

According to a 2016 study coauthored by British anthropologist and evolutionary psychologist Robin Dunbar, most adults shed friends after twenty-five, with men shedding friends at a slightly higher rate.[4] But unlike my friendships with women, where there's usually a reason for the dissolution, like incompatible lifestyles or shifting professional and personal goals, I couldn't find any reasons I'd split with my male friends. We still liked doing the same things—gabbing about our jobs, discussing obscure indie movies, and geeking out over the latest NASA discoveries. As far as I knew, we were still emotionally connected. I couldn't understand why these guy friends were fleeing from me *en masse*.

A 2021 survey conducted by The Survey Center on American Life found that only 43 percent of married women—and 54 percent of married men—say they have a close friend who is a different gender.[5] Meanwhile, nearly two-thirds of unmarried, single women say they have a close male friend. Clearly, marriage is an obstacle that the majority of different-gendered friendships can't overcome.

Shasta Nelson, relationship expert and author of *Frientimacy: How to Deepen Friendships for Lifelong Health and Happiness*, knows how painful these changes in friendships can be. In fact, she says friendships ending often hurts more than romantic relationships coming to an end: "To add to the complexity, the closure isn't as defined or clear as it is when dating someone so the grief can feel more confusing."[6]

When it comes to cross-gender friendships, Nelson says the two most common challenges she hears expressed are: (1) having the courage to have an honest conversation about shared intentions and expectations in the cross-sex friendship to ensure both people are on the same page, and (2) navigating that cross-gender friendship when one or both people are in romantic relationships with others.

According to Nelson, platonic female friends can often be perceived as suspicious, with many women "feeling threatened when it comes to their boyfriends having close female friends." It's a bummer for both women like me, who have this cloud of suspicion over a platonic friendship with a cis-male friend, and women who aren't comfortable with their partners having intimate relationships with other women. We all lose out in this dynamic.

Melissa's Experience

Melissa, a forty-one-year-old mom of two, saw this phenomenon unfold firsthand. In her twenties, her friendships with guys were a glimpse into another world: "When I went on a bad date or had my heart broken, [my guy friends] were able to explain things to me with precision and logic. They helped steer me away from troublesome situations they recognized."

But as she hit her late twenties and early thirties, her friendships with men started falling apart. "As we watched each other become serious about meeting the person we'd like to spend our life with, we failed at making adjustments to our friendship," she recalled.

Henrietta's Experience

Henrietta, a thirty-two-year-old journalist living in New York City, had been friends with Carl since 2007. They attended college together and met while interning at a local TV news station. After thirteen years of friendship, things came to an abrupt end once Carl started dating a new girl who saw a text from Henrietta on his phone.

"My relationship with Carl was never sexual and never went into friends-with-benefits territory, so she really had nothing to be worried about," Henrietta told me via email. "I guess she felt threatened, and he was scared to lose her, so he thought cutting out a friend that he had had for over a decade was a better choice."

Dr. Geoff Greif, author of *Buddy System: Understanding Male Friendships* and distinguished professor at the University of Maryland School of Social

Work, said the biggest problem couples in their late twenties and early thirties face is how they choose to spend their spare time. Between friends, romantic partners, children, other couples, and alone time, something's got to give.

"If I'm going to drop somebody and I don't have a lot of time, I'm going to drop the person that could potentially be most troublesome to my marriage," Dr. Greif told me in an interview.[7] If you're a cis-male, "that's going to be a [friendship with a] woman, perhaps."

Dr. Greif points out that when relationships—platonic and romantic—go south, most men split, as they aren't socialized to fight for friendships. So when friendship issues come up with female friends, men have no clue how to address them.

"I don't know how much training men have had in having a breakup friendship conversation with men, and they certainly have not had it with women. Most of us aren't going to have that conversation," Dr. Greif said. "We're going to let things drift and drag and end in some way."[8]

Maybe my guy friends didn't reject me because they didn't find value in our friendship. They might have just been unequipped to handle those tough conversations because it would put their new romantic relationship in a bad light. And instead of risking conflict with both me and their new partner, they opted to put their partner's feelings first and place our friendship on the back burner.

So are these cross-gender friendships doomed from the start? Do they crumble as soon as we settle down in our thirties? Nelson doesn't think so. "It's appropriate for our relationships to ebb and flow at different times in our lives which means that while our consistency may not be what it used to be, it doesn't mean we can't create a new normal that over time can still be a meaningful support for each of us."[9]

Nelson has some words of encouragement for those that notice their cross-gender friendships waning: "What I think is most important is to remember there are different levels of friendship. I teach [a spectrum of] one to five levels. Remember it's possible that just because we aren't fives anymore doesn't have to mean that we are now zeros. Perhaps we can grieve the loss of the intimacy that came at level five and be grateful that we are still at level three, and know that someday that number can change again. It doesn't have to be all-or-nothing to be meaningful, nor does it need to stay the same."[10]

THERE IS NOTHING EASY ABOUT BEING A FRIEND

Psychologist Eugene Kennedy once wrote, "There is nothing easy about becoming a friend. It requires maturity, self-discipline, and a willingness to be understanding even when we are tired of the effort."

Western culture encourages us to put our immediate needs first. We have unlimited ways to curate the information we expose ourselves to. For example, I'm writing this on an internet browser that's customized to my satisfaction with all my favorite bookmarks displayed in a row, and I'm listening to a playlist of my favorite jazz songs on Spotify.

Friendships aren't anything like these hyper-curated experiences. They demand commitment and sublimation of our selfish desires. We sometimes have to put someone else's needs first, and we often have to consider someone else's limits and preferences. But, Kennedy argued, we should endure the discomfort because the trade-off is worth it. "The sense of ourselves delivered by friendship is unparalleled," he wrote, calling friendship "the affectionate miracle that plunges us into the midst of mystery and reveals the world to us."[11] How beautiful is that? At first, I'm like, "Yes, I'm on board. I want an affectionate miracle!" But then my mind hovers over to the word *mystery*. What is Kennedy talking about?

My theory is that part of the reason for this mystery is that there are no formal ceremonies in adult friendships. In a romantic relationship, you have explicit discussions about your status (Are we dating? Are we exclusive? Will you marry me?) and exclusive labels (boyfriend, girlfriend, spouse, husband, wife, partner, etc.). But there is no "popping the question" in friendships. Most people don't experience anything close to that formality. This ambiguity can create a lot of confusion about the roles friends play in our lives.

Have you ever had someone call you their best friend and you're like, "I had no idea you thought of me like that!" In this way, our adult friendships are an anomaly in our lives. I can't think of any other relationship that has this much ambiguity around it. My sisters know I'm their sister. My husband knows I'm his wife. But I have no clue who considers me their best friend. It's weird, right? We crave stable, positive, and reciprocal friendships, but we have no formal arrangements for them.

THE ANSWER? GET CLARITY ABOUT
THE FRIENDSHIP STATUS

Because our brains hate uncertainty, it's important that you tell your friends that you consider them your friends. Not knowing an outcome stresses us the fuck out, and unpredictable situations require our brains to expend extra energy in order to navigate them. Making sense of the unknown can trigger hormone surges and an increased heart rate. Over time, this chronic stress can negatively impact one's health, increasing the risk for cardiovascular disease and memory loss.

All this confusion around our relationships also leads us to having sky-high expectations of our friendships without ever asking if these expectations are reasonable in the first place. (More on this in chapter 13.) We might feel pain and hurt at expectations that were never properly communicated, but this confusion isn't anyone's fault; it's a shortcoming of our culture that prioritizes career and family over our dear friendships.

The antidote, as the Japanese pole vaulters in chapter 1 knew, is to strive for clarity. Iconic Belgian fashion designer Diane von Furstenberg knows this too. "I can compare clarity to pruning in gardening. You need to be clear," she said. "If you are not clear, nothing is going to happen. You have to be clear. Then you have to be confident about your vision. And after that, you just have to put a lot of work in."[12] She probably wasn't thinking about friendships when she said this, but she's right on the money, as my grandma used to say. You need clarity about why you ache to have close friendships with some people over others, why your friendships are suffering, and how you can give your friendship the best chance to thrive for many years to come.

When you see groups of friends together on social media, you might get the impression that everyone else is having an easy time with their friendships. *They found a way to keep their bonds strong and positive,* you might think. *What's wrong with me? *commence crying into an oat milk latte**

Listen, friendships are complex for everybody. Even the closest, tightest friendships can be challenging at times. They're ambiguous and messy. They're fragile and volatile. But there is a logic to the ups and downs, which is explained through the rubric of Choice Theory and the concept of our unique Quality Worlds.

No matter how we choose our friends, once we have them, it's important to maintain those connections while still leaving time and space to care for ourselves. Mastering this balance is crucial to creating sustainable bonds. One of the ways we can do this is by recognizing friendship tiers and prioritizing interactions accordingly, which is what we'll dive into in the next chapter.

5

Bathtubs, Jacuzzis, and Swimming Pools, Oh My!

We love to talk about self-care in our culture. Bowing out of brunch plans? You're taking time for yourself. Putting your phone on airplane mode to grab peace of mind? You're a self-care hero. But there's a paradox here: if you blow everything (and everyone) off to take care of yourself, how can you still make your friends feel like they are a priority for you?

Perhaps there is a better way to balance your need to be true to yourself with the need to be emotionally available to your friends. To do this, you need to recognize friendship tiers. As you probably know from interacting with people your entire life, not all friendships are equal in intensity. That would be . . . unusual. For the vast majority of us, we enjoy varying degrees of friendship. There are twin flame friendships that have their own secret language, casual nods to acquaintances on the street, and everything in between.

You know those best friend necklaces in the shape of a heart with a line cracking it in half? They're not setting us up for success. I'm sorry to be the one to tell you this, but friendship, as a whole, isn't about two halves of a heart. That story is a fiction, an impossibly high bar to clear. A better necklace would be a pie with pieces that shift in size depending on what's going on in your lives, but I don't think jewelry technology has advanced to that degree. Maybe it could be a hologram. I'm just spitballing here.

I started the book describing the Olympic friendship medal story and bemoaning how we have a lack of clarity in our friendships that creates a lot of confusion. What I propose is that we ask a different question altogether: Can I classify my friends into tiers instead of a ranked position?

If you're old enough to remember the Myspace Top 8, raise your hand. If not, here's a quick rundown: you were given the option to indicate and publicly display your top eight friends on your Myspace profile. Using this same model in real life can be helpful in designating the priorities you should have; however, it can also diminish the importance of the friends you see less frequently.

You, too, might have a compulsion to rank your friends, as if you were living in an episode of *Top Chef* or *Survivor*.

Beth's Experience

"My friends are my allies, cheerleaders, confidants, role models, truth-tellers, and teachers," Beth told me. "I am so grateful to them because they have helped me grow in ways I wouldn't have anticipated." She doesn't always feel completely understood by her family or partner, but she makes up for that by choosing an eclectic group of friends who can relate to her other hobbies, interests, or sense of humor. "I believe that the strong ties also help me be a better daughter, sister, partner, and coworker because there's less strain on those (quasi-involuntary) relationships."

Some people feel their friends are like gardens or concentric circles. Me? I'm inclined to agree with Christian Langkamp. In his book *Practical Friendship*, he encourages us to appreciate the different roles our friends provide for us and acknowledges how appealing it can be to rank our friends.

Instead, Dr. Langkamp encourages us to consider the full scope of what a friendship entails. A friendship isn't egocentric; it's a reciprocal relationship. Yes, we expect a close friend to tend to us when we're in distress, but we must nurture them in return. Yes, we choose our friends, but they have to choose us too.

Instead of rating, scoring, or comparing our friends, Dr. Langkamp feels it's helpful to focus on the roles they play for you, then prioritize them accordingly. After analyzing data he collected on small-scale societies, Dr. Dunbar identified our circles of friendship, which are the layers of connection we have with others.[1] I've rebranded these various groups into tiers that highlight how fluid these groups can be.

Your innermost circle of friends, usually comprising one or two people, are your **Bathtub Friend(s)**. If you're a woman, Dr. Dunbar found, you're likely to have a significant other and one close friend in your bathtub. If you're a man, he found that you're likely to just have your significant other in your bathtub. I hate to make generalizations based on gender (of course, there are always exceptions), but this is what Dr. Dunbar found in his research. This group is called your bathtub friends because, traditionally, there isn't much room in there! This is the closest circle of intimacy with the one or two people you've spent at least two hundred hours of time with. These are the people you would call when you get a scary health diagnosis or have incredible news to share.

Next is your sacred inner circle of two to five buddies, which make up your **Jacuzzi Friends**. Dr. Dunbar calls this our *support clique*. Intimacy in this group is high, and frequency of contact is wicked high, with at least two hundred hours of bonding time. These are the people you rely on for practical and emotional support. You'd pick up the phone for this person at any hour. If you won an Oscar, these people would be the ones you'd thank onstage as you clutched the trophy.

Swimming Pool Friends are the ten to fifteen people who are your "shoulder-to-cry-on" friends. Scientists Christian Buys and Kenneth Larsen call them our sympathy "friends." Maybe you share a passion or a hobby, or they're friends from work or the couples you go on double dates with. There's established trust here, and you'd probably call on them to pet sit, house sit, or watch your kiddo for a few hours. They're someone you've spent up to 200 hours with and have revealed some sensitive, personal things to. Conversation flows freely, and you make a reasonable effort to contact each other sporadically.

Bonfire Friends are the fifty or so friends you have in your contact list. You know basic information about these people as you've spent around 100 hours of bonding time with them. You probably have dozens of bonfire friends just from living your life, going to school, and having a job.

Lastly, are the 150 or so casual **Water Park Friends**, the "weddings and funerals group," Dr. Dunbar called them. These are the dozens of people in your life who would *schlep* themselves to your big, special, once-in-a-lifetime shindig. Over time, these friends can turn into swimming pool friends or deepen into Jacuzzi friends. It's very fluid.

Like good whiskey or cheese, friendships need time to develop depth and richness. As we've learned, it takes about two hundred hours over the course of a few months to promote someone from stranger to close friend. That's why you fell into easy friendships in school or work when you were able to rack up dozens of hours with people with little effort. Finding that time when you're out of school and in the real world—well, that's why friendships fade so easily. The time's just not there to cement the relationship.

Friends can slide from close friends back to friends and even back to acquaintances because they're so expen$ive in terms of time and effort. In fact, according to Dr. Dunbar, falling in love will cost you at least two friendships as your priorities shift and your availability plummets. As a bathtub best friend slips into a Jacuzzi friend, a Jacuzzi friend might get bumped into the swimming pool tier, and so on.

Exercise: Identify Your Pool Partiers

Because we're striving for clarity in our friendships, let's take a snapshot of who is in your life today and identify who you will practice Wholehearted Friendship principles with. These are the people who you will devote the majority of your time, care, and attention to.

Bathtub peeps (one to two people you share the most intimacy with):

Jacuzzi buddies (three to five people in your support group):

_____

Swimming pool (ten to fifteen people in your sympathy group):

_____

These are your core layers of connection at the moment. Keep in mind that these tiers are fluid; people will dip in and out of tiers for any and all reasons. Come back every few months to note how your friend tiers have shifted. This road map will confirm which of your friendships are in a healthy, reciprocal, and functional place. These are the people you prioritize accordingly.

WHEN FRIENDSHIPS FEEL UNBALANCED

A couple years ago, I wrote an article about lopsided friendships for *Vox* and spoke with an unmarried 35-year-old woman named Kristen. She was unhappy because her twelve-year relationship with her best friend, Maria, had become increasingly strained during the pandemic. They were having very different experiences during an incredibly stressful and scary time and were struggling to find common ground. She was clueless about how to make things better. Kristen, a behavioral researcher in San Francisco, was distressingly lonely, as she had no one to hunker down with during the lockdown, leaving her feeling isolated and abandoned.

Maria, also 35, was married and living in Los Angeles. Maria had just given birth to her first child, a girl. Every day brought her new challenges as she navigated being a new mom and wife. Of course, Kristen expected Maria to take some time as she adjusted to these new roles, but she wasn't prepared for how upsetting it would feel to be shuffled to an outer ring of Maria's life precisely when Kristen needed her friend's support and love the most.

Once the baby arrived, the friends made attempts to keep in touch. They scheduled a check-in call every other Sunday at 8 am. At first, Maria was late to their calls but apologetic. After a few months, however, Maria stopped showing up altogether. "She just would get really busy and over-whelmed and forget about me," Kristen told me. With every phone date Maria blew off, Kristen's contempt grew. "It just got so painful that I was like, 'This [friendship] is not working,'" she said. Their friendship had become a swirling pit of sadness and frustration.

Let's analyze what's going on from Kristen's perspective. By mapping out how these big-picture issues affect this particular friendship, we can pinpoint the reasons for the drift and hopefully take the edge off her soreness.

Level of closeness with Maria today: Due to how infrequently they communicate, Kristen and Maria moved from Jacuzzi friends to swimming pool friends and now hover around bonfire friends.

Sociological reason(s) why Kristen's friendship with Maria has been challenging to maintain: Maria married later in life. Both friends moved around a lot. Maria is spending more time with her child than their friendship.

Interpersonal reason(s) why this particular friendship is strained: There has been a downgrade in intensity due to a change in life circumstance (Maria having a child and living far from Kristen).

How this friendship addresses Kristen's five basic needs, according to Choice Theory: Kristen doesn't need Maria's friendship for survival. In fact, the women don't rely on each other in any practical way. Maria contributed to Kristen's greater sense of love and belonging throughout most of their friendship, but Maria hasn't been able to show up in that way for the past year or so. Kristen in San Francisco doesn't derive any power or social standing from this relationship, nor does it enhance her sense of freedom. Lastly, since their interactions aren't especially fun or positive lately, well, it's no wonder Kristen is considering taking space from this valuable friendship.

Insights we now have about the friendship: The friendship is struggling for common, expected reasons. In fact, this strain might have even been inevitable.

My first hope for Kristen is that this exercise will help her see that her friendship is weathering some serious challenges, many that aren't the fault of either person. These are natural, expected changes in long-term, close friendships. My second hope is for Kristen to realize she will need to change her approach to Maria. A standing phone call date wasn't what their friendship needed to stay close. They both needed to offer the other reassurance that even though they won't be able to stay in touch as frequently as they'd like, they still value each other immensely. The intensity of their friendship has changed; they transitioned from Jacuzzi friends to swimming pool and even bonfire friends. Right now, as a new mom, Maria needs flexibility, grace, and understanding. On the flip side, Kristen needs reassurance, kindness, and direct communication.

FRIENDSHIP TIERS INFORM EXPECTATIONS

I recently messaged a friend from high school, "Happy Holidays! I miss you." I didn't hear back for a week. I started to think, *Does she hate me? Does she even want to be in this friendship? Does she not care?*

And then I realized: I'm not in her instant-reply, Jacuzzi tier of friends. I'm probably in her I-will-reply-when-I-have-some-time swimming pool tier. Maybe I've even slid down into her bonfire tier. Then, a calmness washed over me because I now knew how to regard her. It's like going to a restaurant where you enjoyed the food but were annoyed that the service was slow. If I go back to that restaurant, I'll be better prepared. Maybe I'll even bring a book so I won't get annoyed if my grilled cheese takes a half hour to come out from the kitchen. This way, I'm not as peeved at the restaurant for taking forever on my meal; I've adapted my expectations. In fact, if my food comes out at a reasonable time, I'll be pleasantly surprised.

A week after I sent the initial text message, my friend replied with an apology that she took so long to respond. We had a nice, casual chat. I didn't get defensive or take her slow reply personally because I was honest with myself about what kind of friend restaurant I was dining at, so to speak, and I knew how to regard our bond today. Not five years ago. Not five months ago. Today.

It's important to be honest with yourself regarding where you stand with a friend. Sure, you may have been best buds at one point, but life gets complicated. Circumstances change and people change. It's okay to accept that you may now be bonfire friends at best. This level of honesty and acceptance will help adjust your expectations and give you and your friend the opportunity to grow in your friendship at an appropriate pace.

Exercise: Break Out the Bubbly Because It's Awards Season, Baby!

We're taking inventory of our friendships. Not ten years ago. Not last year. Today. So, let's hand out some awards! Jot down the name of whoever in your life comes to mind.

Today's date:

_____

Most likely to answer your text messages within an hour:

_____

Most likely to answer a phone call:

_____

Most likely to make you laugh:

_____

Most likely to help you with a work-related problem:

_____

Most likely to try a new restaurant with you:

_____

Most likely to support your dreams and life goals:

_____

Most likely to let you sleep on their couch:

_____

Most likely to celebrate the holidays with you:

_____

Most likely to motivate you:

_____

Most likely to give you useful health advice:

_____

Most likely to give you wise romantic advice:

_____

Most likely to give you sound financial advice:

_____

Most likely to be in your life in a year:

_____

Most likely to confide a secret in you:

_____

Most likely to celebrate a professional accomplishment with you:

_____

Most likely to give you good TV/movie/music/podcast recommendations:

_____

Most likely to sit with you in comfortable silence:

_____

Most likely to suggest a good book you'll enjoy:

_____

Most likely to discuss politics with you:

_____

Most likely to offer you a long hug when you need one:

_____

After completing this exercise, think about how this activity makes you feel about who you listed. Are you surprised? Sad? Conflicted? Thankful? You might be surprised to see the names of children, older relatives, or people you didn't even consider as friends on this list.

6

Why We Have the Friends We Do

I'm an impulsive lady. My whims, desires, and impulses have resulted in all types of fiascos like near-empty bank accounts, drawers full of not-right lipsticks, and dozens of mediocre hookups across the tristate area.

I will say that my impulses have certainly made my life more interesting. Junior year of high school, I once pretended one of my contact lenses was scratched. I winced in pain, rapidly blinked my right eye, and asked the teacher if I could head to the bathroom to investigate. Of course, she agreed because my acting skills were incredible.

Once I left the classroom, I strolled the halls, happy to have a break from the monotony of the day. Four minutes into my walkabout, I ran into an acquaintance named Sari. She laughed when I told her what I was doing, and then asked if I had any plans that weekend. There was a punk show downtown and I was welcome to join her and a few of her friends. I said I'd love to go, and that choice (not to be dramatic) CHANGED MY ENTIRE LIFE. Not only did I become best friends with one of the other girls who joined us that night, but I soon became heavily involved in the local Chicago punk scene. I started going to punk shows every weekend, which led to my meeting my first boyfriend, along with all sorts of wonderful people whom I still call friends to this day.

All this from impulsively faking an injury. In this case, my impulsivity, my willingness to try something new, worked out for me.

Impulsivity has also bitten me in the ass. A few years ago, when I was still single, one of my closest friendships with a woman named Julia imploded. I hadn't been friends with Julia that long, only a year or two, but we hit it off right away. I met her at a Philly house party, where she was dressed like a French pop star from the '60s: sweeping, black-licorice-colored bangs; minimal makeup; a cream-colored pleated skirt; and a simple, prim, black button-up cardigan. Like me, she was boy crazy. In fact, she'd briefly dated a local musician with whom I was semi-obsessed. I eagerly ate up all the details she shared about him ("a cheapskate mouth breather who snores like a walrus"), and my response was basically, "When can we hang out again, and can it be tomorrow?"

Our blossoming friendship was like slipping into a warm bath. We fit together so well. Like me, she was Jewish, knew her way around a dive bar jukebox, and used to live in New York City. We would joke that we were basically sisters from other misters. Julia's friendship made me bolder, more confident. I watched her walk into a room with her head up and her back straight. I started walking straighter too. She made me feel like we were in a special girl gang of sassy Jewish chicks.

But Julia turned my world upside down when she hooked up with my best friend, Gabe. I had confided in Julia that I had a crush on Gabe, whom I'd met three years prior at an indie rock show. Gabe had just moved to Philly from Seattle. He was intelligent, funny, and sweet. I wasn't attracted to him right away. But as we deepened our friendship, I saw sides of his personality that appealed to me. He was practical, direct. He kept his word. He was trustworthy.

After a particular gnarly breakup, I leaned on Gabe a little too much. Late-night hangouts at local bars became more frequent, and by my third beer of the night, my eyes would soften and my pulse would race. Slowly Gabe started to look pretty good on the barstool next to me. Perhaps, I wondered, he would be a safe place for my wounded heart.

Julia knew I struggled with that attraction because I didn't want to jeopardize my friendship with him. I introduced Julia to Gabe one Sunday at brunch. To my horror, they hit it off. In fact, after flirting for a solid hour, they left the restaurant to go back to his place and hook up. I was stunned. Julia knew I had feelings for Gabe, but she didn't seem to care. She didn't even hesitate to leave brunch with him. She agreed instantly. Their romance felt like a betrayal. I couldn't handle talking to her (or him) as I processed what was happening. The entire fling made me feel rotten, like my feelings didn't matter to her.

Gabe couldn't understand why I was so upset that he wanted to date Julia. I had to swallow my pride and explain to him that I had feelings for him, which Julia knew. I explained how it hurt to see them together. I felt rejected by him, unknowingly, and undermined by Julia, knowingly. This conversation required such an insane amount of vulnerability on my part that, by the end of our talk, I wanted to transform into a balloon and float away. To his credit, Gabe was wonderfully sensitive to my situation. He explained how he and I would never date because he viewed me more like a sister, a best friend. I asked for space to heal my wounded ego, which he was happy to give. He let me know he was there for me when I was ready to resume our friendship.

In contrast, Julia was floored by my response to her hookup with Gabe. To her, she didn't feel like I had any right to dictate whom she could date. Our friendship was separate from her dating life, she told me. We were at a standstill. Her relationship with Gabe only lasted a couple of months, but our friendship was over. I couldn't understand how she chose this short-term romantic relationship over our friendship. She couldn't understand why I couldn't be happy that she'd met a great guy.

On an individual level, Julia and I had incredible chemistry. We both were silly brunettes who loved *Twin Peaks*, Joy Division, and cats. We also had geographical factors in our favor: we both lived in Philly, so it was easy to see each other regularly. We diverged from one another, on one core value: loyalty.

Her decision to hook up with Gabe strained our bond beyond a breaking point. We tried to become friends again a few years later, but the damage was done. I felt like I could never fully trust her again, and she felt like I wasn't able to forgive her fully. It was really sad, and it still is today.

But this is a great example of how essential it is to share the same values with your friends. Let's revisit the top five reasons friendships crumble, which we covered in chapter 1:

1. Someone moves away

2. Mismatch of values and opinions

3. Downgrade due to a change in life circumstance

4. Conflict of some sort

5. Drifting due to a change in personality or lifestyle

A mismatch in core values is RIGHT THERE as one of the top reasons friendships end. So yeah, making sure your values align is a pretty important component to practicing wholehearted relationships.

WHERE TO FIND FRIENDS

If you're thinking, *Where do I find these magical new friends who align with my values?* The answer is that they're everywhere around you. There's no shortage of opportunities to meet new people. Think of the places you go physically and virtually. According to The Survey Center on American Life, people tend to make close friends at work or school, through an existing network of friends or a close friend in their neighborhood, or at their place of worship or a club or organization they belong to.[1]

As we've previously discussed, we sometimes keep friends around because we've already invested so much time in the relationship. By default, your best friend is the person who's known you the longest and has been by your side through life's ups and downs.

Of course, there is value in having friends who have known so many versions of you. They know which town you grew up in, they've likely met your zany relatives, and they've seen you navigate vicious heartbreaks. These friends have witnessed you overcome challenges at work and school, and they've seen your triumphs too, like running your first marathon or starting an Etsy business. But you may find that just because you've had a friend for a long time, it doesn't mean you're a perfect fit forever.

INDIVIDUAL AND ENVIRONMENTAL FACTORS

We generally choose our friends based on two categories: individual factors and environmental factors.[2] Individual factors are variables like approachability (how friendly you seem), social skills (how friendly you actually are), self-disclosure (your ability to reveal vulnerable things about yourself), similarity (common interests), and closeness (how well you both vibe). These traits vary from person to person. You may meet a group of people in your pottery class, but you might hit it off on a friend level with only one or two people.

Sparkling interpersonal chemistry is what makes friendships feel special. Snoop Dogg and Martha Stewart have superb chemistry. So do the Golden Girls. Maybe you find someone easy to talk to or very welcoming. Or you find them interesting and appealing in some way. Perhaps you also find them attractive. In the instance of friendships, attraction isn't just about looks; it can be about another person's demeanor or warmth.

I met my best friend Lynn in a South Philly alley outside a basement punk show. The year was 2002, and I had just moved to Philly from Brooklyn and didn't know a soul. Lynn was wearing a black-and-white polka-dot dress and had on fiery red lipstick, which I found enchanting. We struck up a conversation, and she invited me to a student fashion show she was putting on at her school. We both were creative people living in Philly, me with my music writing and her with fashion design. As we got to know each other better, I saw she was hilarious and intelligent too. But it was that initial impression, that zing of attraction, that made me open to exploring a friendship with her.

On the other hand, environmental factors are things like proximity (physical nearness to one another, like sitting next to each other in class), geography (living close to one another), activities (things you do together), and life events (navigating similar life stages together). These are the variables that are unique to where two friends both physically reside and are in their lives. In my case, I met Lynn at a local punk show (proximity), and we started hanging out regularly because we both lived in Philly (geography).

The Propinquity Effect—from the Latin word *propinquitas*, which means "nearness"—states that the closer in proximity you are to someone, the more likely you are to have a fondness for them. If you live on the third floor of your college dorm, you're more likely to befriend other people who live on the third floor.

Milestone events also have a strong impact on the kinds of friendships you seek out. When you become engaged, you might gravitate toward friends who are also engaged or newly married. They can give you practical support (go with this wedding venue and not that one) and emotional support (there's a lot of pressure to honor multiple families in a wedding) in a way an unmarried friend may not necessarily be attuned to.

Or, when you have a child, you might find yourself seeking out advice and camaraderie with other friends who are parents. You can ask which doulas are best and which day care facilities are a good fit. If you take up marathon running, you might seek out others in your orbit who also run around on purpose (I can't relate!). It's natural to want to bring in those who can support you in the specific way you need it.

Speaking of milestones, have you experienced any of the following in the past few years?

- Entering a new romantic relationship
- Getting engaged
- Getting married
- Moving
- Losing or changing jobs
- Getting a promotion at work
- Experiencing a death in the family
- Experiencing a birth in the family
- Adopting new pets
- Significant financial changes
- Going back to school
- Graduating from school

- Betrayal or a catastrophe

- Fertility problems

- Treatment for a mental or physical illness

- Hospitalization

- Living through a global pandemic (go ahead and circle this one)

- Other ginormous life changes

It's very normal to seek out those who can support you as you go through milestone events. But if your bond is forged over the event, you may find it hard to keep the friendship afloat when you aren't in the same headspace anymore. It's hard to keep up with my friends from grad school now that we've graduated and are back to our "real" lives. And similarly, you may not keep in touch with the women in your infertility support group once you have children.

But it's not just about feeling loved and supported, social psychologist Carolyn Weisz told me. It's also about feeling understood and respected for who you are. And the practical application of knowing this.

"Of course, you want your friends to make you feel loved and accepted," Dr. Weisz told me.[3] "But I have people who love and accept me, and I don't want that friendship from them," she said. Sometimes unwanted friendship feels like a burden. "In that way, it's a double-edged sword to have people who really love you who you actually don't click with," she said.

Of course, we all want to be loved and accepted, but friendship is often more complicated than that. As people begin careers and find themselves having to select who to spend time with or not, "the identity support piece helps to explain some of the challenging selectivity that can happen in friendships as friendships fade away and new ones form," Dr. Weisz said.

Exercise: Identify Places to Make Friends

If you're open to meeting new people, you may not know where to start, especially if you moved to a new town. Mark anything you'd feel comfortable doing.

_____ Join a gym or walking club

_____ Join an alumna group

_____ Take yoga or fitness classes

_____ Volunteer for charities close to your heart

_____ Join a Facebook group for fans of a favorite podcast or TV show

_____ Search for interesting, like-minded people in your industry on LinkedIn

_____ Start a local chapter of a national organization you're passionate about

_____ Attend local literary events for your favorite author

_____ Join a coworking space a few times a month

_____ Get involved at your church or synagogue

_____ Find other people who love your favorite musical artist

_____ Take an improv class

_____ Start a club focused around a food or beverage you're passionate about (think: organic wine tasting, pizza parties, etc.)

_____ Volunteer at a local museum

_____ Volunteer for a local political campaign

_____ Start a newsletter or podcast about something you're obsessed with

_____ Go to a Comic-Con event

_____ Organize an alcohol-free happy hour at a local park or café and invite a handful of people you'd like to get to know better

_____ Attend local farmers markets and chat with anyone who seems nice

_____ Go to a concert by yourself. Say hi to anyone who seems friendly.

The more things you're willing to do, the more likely you'll meet people who share a passion similar to yours.

These are just a few of the ways people meet friends in their community. As you enter these spaces, you're going to meet all sorts of people. So how do you identify the most promising candidates? How do you pick which friends to invite into your world for good? That's where our intuition comes into play, which we'll explore more in the next chapter.

7

Can We Trust Our Intuition When Picking Friends?

I was standing in line at Dominique Ansel's bakery in the Lower East Side of Manhattan when panic set in. If you haven't heard of Mr. Ansel, he's the trim Frenchman who invented the cronut, a croissant-donut hybrid. If Freddy Mercury and Willy Wonka had a love child, he would be Dominique Ansel.

I squeaked into the cafe at 7:45 pm on a Tuesday night, fifteen minutes before closing time. The staff had already locked the front door and were trying to finish their last few orders of the day. I was in the Mecca of goo-filled pastries. Behind a glass partition were rows upon rows of god-level baked goods. Of course, I wanted to try everything.

When the petite saleslady asked what I wanted, I didn't give an order as much as I unleashed a stream-of-consciousness wish list. I requested anything that sounded sticky, custardy, or decadent.

Ultimately, I ordered about ten items: a salted caramel eclair, a Kouign-Amann, a handful of Canelé de Bordeaux, mini madeleines, and a sickly sweet strawberry cronut. There was no universe in which I could have eaten these pastries in one, two, or even five sittings. It was too much. Too expensive. Too WTF-bonkers.

I'm not proud of this incident because it highlights several of my flaws: I'm impulsive, I make weird decisions with money, and I have crappy self-control. But this is a useful example of how someone might think when they're flustered or excited. With so much information coming in, people have to employ some way to cut through the noise and make a decision, just as I did.

This is where intuition comes in. I make most of my decisions the same way I chose that battalion of pastries at closing time: I listen to my innermost desires. But is trusting our gut really the best way to make decisions? How reliable is our intuition when it comes to other decisions like choosing a job, enrolling in a school, or picking a friend at a Philly house party?

I'm putting it out there: trusting your gut can be dicey because you might be making choices with incomplete information. (For the record, I barely made a dent in the fleet of baked goods. I took four bites of the cronut before I gave myself a bellyache.) But perhaps it would help to start by defining what exactly intuition is.

Generally speaking, intuition is an emotionally charged, rapid, nonconscious processing of emotional information, a positive or negative feeling you have that's instinctual (a hunch) rather than rational (a logical analysis). "Often referred to as 'gut feelings,' intuition tends to arise holistically and quickly, without awareness of the underlying mental processing of information," according to *Psychology Today*.[1] They're hunches, quick assessments.

A 2016 study found that people executed tasks faster, better, and with more confidence when led by their intuition.[2] So far, my intuition has been responsible for:

- Purchasing a Joey McIntyre T-shirt at a New Kids on the Block (NKOTB) concert in sixth grade

- Wearing only black T-shirts

- Ordering the fish special at an Italian restaurant

In each of these cases, I didn't deliberate when making these choices. I didn't poll family and friends about what I should do. I didn't consult a psychic or flip a coin. I just knew that I wanted these things instinctively because Joey was the cutest NKOTB member, black T-shirts don't show stains, and a branzino special sounds damn tasty.

Daniel Kahneman, a Nobel Prize–winning psychologist and researcher, theorized that we have two distinct thought systems when it comes to intuition.[3] The first system, called **the intuitive system**, is our sixth sense. It's fast and subconscious, which is useful when you need to make split-second decisions. This hunch helps us sidestep threats in a chaotic world (hiring the wrong person to babysit our kid) and pounce on opportunities (introducing ourselves to a promising new friend). But the intuitive system is more prone to error and biases, as it's essentially a best guess at the moment.

Examples of intuitive thinking:

- Taking a different route to work
- Saying yes to a second date
- Accepting (or declining) a job
- Deciding what to wear today

The second system, called **the analytical system**, is slower and more fastidious. This one engages higher, more complex reasoning. This system helps you make wiser decisions. It's the older sibling counseling you to slow down and think things through.

Generally, these two systems happen at the same time. Experience has taught you that men with wallet chains make lousy boyfriends, so you're less likely to be open to a guy hitting on you if you notice chunky-ass steel links hanging from his baggy pants. It's what happens when clocking a quick impression merges with the wealth of evidence you've accumulated from past experience.

So, what does intuition have to do with Wholehearted Friendship? Well, if you have friends whom you picked based on intuition alone when you were younger, your friendship with this person may be based on incomplete or outdated information.

Do you ever wonder if you'd initiate a friendship with a longtime friend if you met each other today, knowing what you now know about their lifestyle or value system? Do you still feel like the other person is a good fit? It's understandable if you've never given much thought to why you gravitate toward your friends. When you have so much history together, it might even feel strange or cruel to question whether someone is an appropriate friend for you today.

To that I'd say: a wholehearted friend takes the time to understand exactly why their friendships are working for them. It's important to be smart about the people we let into our lives. Who you live with, who you work with, who you date—these decisions impact your life in countless ways. Friends can influence your physical and emotional health, and they can expand or limit your opportunities.

Socrates is believed to have said, "Be slow to fall into friendship; but when thou art in, continue firm and constant."[4] He understood, I assume, that friendship shouldn't be something you dive into willy-nilly. Caution and calmness are important so you can discern what the other person's deal is. It might be new for you to think about friendships in terms of how they can help or hurt you. It might even feel sacrilegious to dissect a friendship like this, like you're being clinical or heartless. But if you're frustrated or unhappy with your friendships, it's an exercise worth doing. By articulating who's a good candidate for friendship and why, you might also understand why some people may not be as good of a match. Mismatches won't make friendship impossible, but it helps to be aware of potential issues so you can proceed wisely.

Another benefit of surrounding yourself with wonderful friends is that you will be able to teach, encourage, and grow with the people who bring out your best qualities. But relying on intuition alone may not be the best way to discern if a friend is compatible with you. You need to get the full measure of a person before you call them a close friend.

When writing on the beauty of imperfection, Eugene Kennedy said, "If you ask people what attracted them to the person they love, they never tell you of some perfect feature that focused them on sheer surfaces but rather an imperfection that allowed them to see into their uncharted depths."[5] The issue many of us with long-standing friendships have is distinguishing between which imperfections are permissible and which ones should make you slow your roll, as Socrates warned us. Imperfections are important. We all have 'em. And there's allure there. But there's a difference between quirks and cringy behaviors that leave you feeling disrespected.

Many times, you may not be aware that your values clash with a friend until it's too late, as I discovered with Julia. Moving forward, it's important that you're clear about your values so you can be more attuned if you sense a friend isn't on the same page.

I now see that I might have overlooked some signs that Julia and I weren't on the same page. The first clue: all throughout our short friendship, she kept remarking about how wild it was that she enjoyed hanging out with me because she normally didn't get along with other women. I remember thinking, *That's strange*, but I didn't dwell on it. If anything, I felt proud of myself. Somehow, unlike any other woman on the planet, I made her feel so loved and understood. I must be a SUPER GREAT friend if she would want to be my friend.

I once asked her to elaborate on why she didn't connect with more women. She told me she had a spotty track record of being friends with ladies. They were usually catty with her and didn't seem to like her very much. I was naive and assumed it'd be different with us. If anything, I took this as evidence that our friendship was strong and special.

Now I realize that she had a history of disregarding friends' feelings when it came to issues of romance. Julia looked out for Julia. That's how she was. I didn't really understand what she meant about not getting along with other women until I saw her vibing with my crush Gabe. Then it was like a giant light bulb lit up over my head: *Oh, that's what she meant when she says other women don't like her.* It's because she prioritizes herself and her feelings. She doesn't care whom she hurts to get what she wants. That's what she was trying to tell me.

That situation let me know how important loyalty is to me in a friendship. So today, I make sure that the friends I choose have their own history of trustworthy behavior in their friendships. In fact, when I met my friend Allison, we took our time developing our friendship, building up good habits over months and years. I've met Allison's other friends and see that she's a loyal, thoughtful person who is a fantastic friend to others in her life. I feel safe with her, like she's a smart person to trust. We have a whole-hearted friendship; we give each other grace, care, and respect.

Note if your former friends didn't share your key values. Take a beat and reflect on that information. Let's revisit the sentiment of Socrates again. It makes sense to be cautious as you discern if your values are compatible. But the second part of his advice is about staying firm and constant. Let's explore that for a beat. Be slow in order to assure your values align. Be firm and constant by understanding why your friendship works.

Exercise: Identify Your Values as a Friend

Name three to six values you hold in a friendship. What qualities are essential to you in your close friendships? Respect, kindness, open-mindedness, generosity, loyalty, curiosity, adventurousness, independence, good communication, a wicked good sense of humor, empathy? Think deeply about which qualities are essential for you to feel compatible with a friend.

_____

_____

_____

_____

_____

For me, my values are being caring, open-minded, respectful, generous, and creative. So if I value respect and see a potential friend talk down to a server, you can understand why I might want to distance myself from this person. If I value open-mindedness and have a friend who refuses to try new restaurants or deviate from our routine, that could dissuade me from wanting to go out with her more.

Think of friends you've had in your past. Where did your values align? Where did they diverge? How did the values you independently held impact your friendship's health?

Our intuition is an imperfect mechanism, but it is through this innate ability that we are able to initially evaluate others. Wholehearted Friendship is about taking all the information we have about a person into account when we decide to become friends with them. If you have friends you chose when you were younger, your relationship may not have evolved as you've evolved. This is an issue because sharing similar values is crucial to having a solid foundation in a relationship. Becoming clear on the values you hold will help you better assess who would be a good candidate to be friends with. Those select people will comprise your trusted inner circle. More on that in the next chapter.

8

Happy People Do This One Thing Instinctively

I n his book *Vital Friends: The People You Can't Afford to Live Without*, author Tom Rath says we ideally should have a variety of friends who support us in specific ways.[1] No one friend can be everything to you. And you shouldn't carry that expectation. Instead, we should cultivate different types of friends who excel at certain complementary behaviors. "Friendships are not designed to be well-rounded; 83% of the people we have studied report that they bring different strengths to the relationship than their best friend does," Rath wrote, stressing that we should not expect any of our friends to be good at everything.[2] Rather, he says the key to wonderful friendships is focusing on what each friend uniquely contributes to your life.

Elaine's Experience
Elaine said that her friends share two qualities: (1) they are not boring, and (2) they are affirming. She loves when friends surprise her by asking interesting questions and making her laugh in creative and new ways. "People who are interested in the things you find fundamentally interesting and show you how previously mundane things are actually worth hours of conversation," she said.

The second quality is fuzzier. When she says affirming, she doesn't mean she needs her friends to validate her feelings and perspective. "It goes beyond someone who agrees with you. I have friends who I know disagree with me, but they make me feel seen, they listen, and they affirm that they are there with me, even if they don't always understand or we can't exactly agree on what 'there' is."

In ice cream terms, vanilla will always be vanilla. It doesn't do a great job at being pistachio. If you want to have a rockin' sundae bar (i.e., healthy, functional friendships), you're going to need different flavors of ice cream. A scoop of mint cookie, a scoop of butter pecan, a scoop of raspberry ripple, and so on. Friends are the exact same way. Your friend who isn't great at celebrating your professional successes is not going to suddenly change one day and congratulate you on your job promotion. If you're looking for a friend to high-five you about a success at work, share your good news with the friends in your life who are able to take joy in celebrating your career milestones.

Friends do many things for us: they care about us, they celebrate our successes, they make us laugh, they offer support and encouragement. But it's not realistic to have one person do all these things perfectly every time.

Rath came up with core roles that your most vital friends can play in your life. He defines a vital friend as someone who measurably improves your life AND a person at work or in your personal life whom you can't afford to live without. To discern if someone should be classified as a vital friend, he says you should ask yourself a couple questions: If this person were no longer around, would your overall satisfaction with life decrease? And, if this person were no longer a part of your life, would your achievement or engagement at work decrease? If you can answer yes to either or both of these questions, then congrats, you have a vital friend! *throws a handful of confetti in the air*

The vital roles that Rath outlines describe what the person brings into the friendship: the energy, the strengths, the positives. Sometimes, friends can play the same role in each other's life (coworkers being each other's champions). Sometimes, friends provide totally different roles for one another (a free spirit opens the other person's mind, the dependable friend provides companionship). As long as each friend considers the other person a vital player in their life, it can be a positive relationship.

The vital role assignment always comes *after* the reason for the friendship is established. If the purpose of the friendship is compelling enough to both people, that friend will have a chance of becoming a vital friend to you.

People have significantly better friendships if they can easily describe what each friend contributes to the relationship. Here are the eight most common friendship roles Rath's research identified:[3]

Builders have coach energy. They want you to succeed in all you do. This friend motivates you, invests in your personal or professional development, and truly wants you to come out on top. There's no sense of competition evident with a builder. Instead, this person aims to complement and support your goals.

Champions are your personal cheerleaders. They sing your praises to others, have your back, and will advocate for you even when you're not around. Champions accept you for who you are and don't judge you. Champions are your strongest, most loyal supporters who are psyched about your accomplishments and truly want you to find happiness.

Collaborators are friends who dig the same hobbies and passions as you. Want to try a new brunch spot or attend a workshop together? Your collaborator will be right there, stoked to try it out with you and compare notes. You have similar ambitions in both work and life. You have a strong bond and a similar relationship to your shared passions. Maybe you're both in the same club or organization.

Companions are always there for you, whatever the circumstances. You share a bond that is virtually unbreakable. When something big happens in your life—good or bad—these are the people you call first. Companions take pride in your relationship, and they will sacrifice for your benefit. These are the friends for whom you might literally put your life on the line.

Connectors are the resource-minded people who help you get what you want. These friends get to know you and then instantly work to connect you with others who will share your interests or goals. They extend your network dramatically and give you access to new means. If you need a job, a doctor, a friend, or a date, call a Connector.

Energizers are your fun-as-hell friends who always boost your spirits and create more positive moments in your life. Energizers have a remarkable ability to figure out what gets you going. They pick you up when you're feeling down and can turn a good day into an incredible one. Call on your Energizers when you need a laugh, a smile, or some good vibes.

Mind Openers expand your horizons and introduce you to new ideas, opportunities, cultures, and people. They challenge you to think in innovative ways and help you create lasting, positive change. They know how to ask great questions that make you more receptive to ideas. Mind Openers challenge conventional wisdom and allow you to express opinions you might be uncomfortable articulating to others.

Navigators are friends who give you fantastic, relevant advice and keep you headed in the right direction. You seek them out when you need guidance. They're wonderful at talking you through your options. If you are in a difficult situation or at a crossroads, talk to a Navigator. They are best at hearing your dreams and goals and then helping you find the path to achieve them.

When considering your own vital friends, think about how they achieved that title. Did you consciously think, *I really need an energizer in my life; let me seek out someone who cracks me up*? Most likely not! You probably were in their orbit, hit it off, spent loads of time with them doing something you both were passionate about, then realized that this person fills a vital role for you.

If you're struggling with the loss of a special friendship, it might be because this person was a vital friend to you. Losing this person's presence in your life is distressing. It creates a void because they feel irreplaceable.

More specifically, you have not just lost a friend, but the crucial role they played in your life.

Wholehearted Friendship is all about embracing this clarity, knowing how and why you choose the friends you do and why you specifically need them in your life. It's like figuring out what genres of music you like or what kinds of video games you prefer playing. This is key information about yourself and why you gravitate toward the things you do. Learning about vital roles is a superb way to understand what each friend contributes and how they influence you. It puts into words what you might already know: some friends are better suited for sharing certain parts of your life. Some friends are better for lending a sympathetic ear. Other friends are happy to pop some bottles and dance the pain away with you.

These vital roles also emphasize balance; one person can't be everything to us. We NEED a cast of people who can support us effectively (and who *you* can support effectively).

Olivia's Experience

Olivia sees her friendships as supplements to her marriage, which feels healthier for her. "If you want a nice, normal guy who's going to be supportive and understanding and a good listener, you can't demand that they then also take all your emotional needs, all your fun and entertainment needs, all your like chit-chat needs," she said. "It's just too much, and it doesn't leave any room in the relationship for breathing or freshness."

She used to be envious of her friends who had those relationships: "I've realized over the years to shift those needs to other people who are more receptive to them." She needs other people to fill those roles and feels it's disrespectful to one's partner to expect them alone to give you that energy you crave.

Your friendships are precious, and that's why it's important to use your intuition, hold true to your values, and identify the unique role a friend plays in your life. By tapping into all three facets, you can understand precisely why you have the friends you do. Consequently, you can better evaluate whether a friendship is, or is not, an adequate fit for your life today.

....

Exercise: Cast Your Friendship Roles

Identify who in your life plays these roles for you.

Builders:

_____

Champions:

_____

Collaborators:

_____

Companions:

_____

Connectors:

_____

Energizers:

_____

Mind Openers:

_____

Navigators:

_____

If you're reeling from friendship breakups, identify what role(s) those friends played for you.

Name of friend:

_____

Role:

_____

Name of friend:

_____

Role:

_____

Name of friend:

_____

Role:

_____

Reflect on how this knowledge makes you feel:

_____

Generally speaking, people who can easily describe what role each friend plays in their lives tend to have better friendships. This is because clarity imparts purpose, establishing a clear and compelling reason why both people seek one another out and continue to put in the work to maintain the friendship.

In the next chapter, we'll shift gears to uncover the various reasons why friendships fail, because while it's important to understand why these bonds form, it's also important to learn why—and how—they fracture.

9

Why Friendships Fail

In 2007, a typical weekend for me looked like: drinking as my friends and I got ready to go out, drinking as we waited for the cab to come pick us up, and drinking as we partied at Philly's dingiest nightclubs. Jack and Cokes to start. Long Island iced teas (in pint glasses) when I wanted to ride out the buzz.

In this swirl of partying, I put up a free ad on Craigslist looking for a roommate to share my two-bedroom apartment in the Fairmount neighborhood of Philadelphia. My ad, admittedly, was bare bones. I think I wrote something like, "Please be a cool person. Don't be boring or messy."

Brielle responded to my semi-deranged classified ad. I looked her up on Myspace and realized we had several friends in common. She went to college with some people I'd known while living in New York City. This was thrilling for me. Although Brielle didn't end up moving in with me—she picked a place closer to her grad school twenty minutes away—we fell into an easy friendship. She was intelligent and tough, a bulldozer with a pixie haircut.

The first time we hung out, we grabbed four-dollar happy hour margaritas at a Philly dive bar called The Ministry of Information. This place was a birdbath for chronically underemployed indie band dudes—and no, not the pouty, raggedly handsome lead singers. This dive was a clubhouse for the more socially awkward bassists and drummers.

Inside the bar, the lighting was soft and yellowish, which made it feel like it was dipped in honey. Broke, shaggy-haired dudes milled about (all named Matt, Adam, or Noah), congregating around the pool table and nursing Red Stripes as they mumbled jokes to one another. None of these Matts, Adams, or Noahs ever made us girls laugh, though. They reminded me of roughly used shower poufs in that their best days were definitely behind them.

Brielle emailed me suggesting we meet up on a brisk Wednesday in early March, as she had a crush on a blond bartender at the Ministry named Todd. She asked if I wanted to swing by and stare at Todd with her. I said sure because I'm always keen to stare at an above-average-looking man pouring alcoholic drinks. The fact that I'd get to do it with a promising new friend like Brielle was an irresistible offer. I was happy to play wingwoman. Our first friend date was set.

We arrived separately at 5 pm and stayed until closing time at 2 am. That night, we came up with no less than ten new inside jokes with each other. One was about sitting on a barstool wearing too-short skirts. Another was about how I was attracted to men who reminded me of the '80s movie actor Dudley Moore. Neither of us wanted the night to end, so we kept ordering round after round of drinks. We took a cab back to my apartment, where she snoozed on my overstuffed apple-fritter-brown sectional.

The next morning, to combat our wicked hangovers, we scarfed down bacon, egg, and cheese bagels from Dunkin' Donuts. It helped soak up some of the alcohol that was no doubt still in our systems. We locked eyes as we sank our teeth into our respective bagel sandwiches, and we both instinctively knew the foundation for our friendship was cemented.

After that night, we were inseparable. In fact, for the majority of our intense three-year friendship, being Brielle's best friend was a total delight. She was side-splitting, wet-your-pants hilarious. She was artistic, creative, and magnetic. Almost every guy I knew had a crush on her.

She'd write me text messages like, "You're the best! I'm so glad I have you in my life. Not to be all cheesy, but I really don't know what I'd do without you! I love you so much!"

We'd sip mugs of Jameson-splashed hot toddies together in her kitchen on chilly days. I'd leave her house with small jars of cinnamon applesauce and peach jam, presents she made for me out of love. She'd encourage me to go after my dream of being a writer and made me feel lovable. Valued, even.

Our differences complemented each other, and our similarities made me feel electric. For instance, we had opposite tastes in men, so we never competed on that front, THANK GOD. I preferred short-statured, nervous, squirrely guys; and she lusted after the tall, lanky, brooding dudes. My fellas would sip dark IPAs and order a bacon cheeseburger. Her guys would order matcha lattes and a hummus plate.

Cracks emerged in our bond a year later as Brielle's facade fell bit by bit. She was suspicious of new friends I'd make or guys I'd date. The things I initially liked about her—her unrelenting ambition, her fierce independence, her ability to not care what other people think—became pain points in our friendship.

The soaring ambition transformed into a troubling competitiveness between us. The fierce independence warped into her overstepping my boundaries. Her ability not to care what people think meant she also didn't seem to care how her actions and words affected me, her supposed best friend.

Her troubling, controlling, entitled behavior was a slow gas leak that poisoned both of us. This was because Brielle felt that I, as her best friend, should be available to her at all times. If I wasn't available—say, I was out with another friend or taking a midday power nap—she'd track me down like she was Liam Neeson and I was her missing teenage daughter. If I didn't answer her first phone call, she'd keep calling me every four minutes. Then a barrage of texts would roll in: "Hey, I called you. Where are you?" Then she'd email me: "Call me." Our friendship was exhausting, stifling.

I started to not like who I was becoming when we were together. I'd feel smaller, resigned, browbeaten. It didn't even feel like we were in a partnership anymore; her emotions and needs felt like the only ones that mattered.

I spent increasing amounts of energy placating her. It was easier to go along with Brielle's wishes ("Fine, we'll go to the house party across town to see your crush") than try to advocate for myself and my desires ("Honestly,

I'd rather not watch you chase yet another emotionally unavailable part-time deejay").

She was stubborn and full of pride. My Old Navy clothes were too cheap looking, she said. My taste in music was too pop-punky. She'd ridicule the quiet guys I dated. She even bullied me into breaking up with a few of them, as she insisted that they weren't "good enough" for me. Good enough for what? Having a beer together on a Tuesday night? WHATEVER, BRIELLE.

If you'd ask me if I was in a toxic friendship with her at the time (circa 2010-ish at this point), I'd deny it too hard. Then, I'd rebrand her worst traits: She wasn't insensitive; she was misunderstood. She wasn't entitled; she just knew her worth. She wasn't cutting; she just had a dark sense of humor. Then, I'd list her positive attributes: she was loyal, engaged, opinionated.

Things came to a head on a warm June afternoon. Brielle muscled in on my plans with a new friend. It was embarrassing. But it was the physical sensation of dread at seeing her name on my phone that let me know that our friendship was ruptured. I didn't have the fortitude (?) or bravery (?) to confront her. It was like asking me to reason with a tornado.

Brielle wasn't invited to Lily's house that day, but as we've established, Brielle didn't care about what others thought of her. I'm sure if you asked her, she would reply that if I was invited, as my best friend, she felt automatically invited too. She even invited herself on whole-ass vacations I'd taken. She would pump me for info about the trip—When are you going? Which airline? Where are you staying?—then she'd just decide to attend without asking me. She tagged along when I visited a good friend of mine in Chicago and foisted herself into joining my trip to see a pal in D.C.

Feeling trapped, I complained about Brielle to my other friends. Venting felt good in the moment, but ultimately, these venting sessions didn't do anything to change my situation. None of my other friends knew what to tell me. They didn't want to incur Brielle's wrath either. If I were to grow a backbone and confront her about how unhappy I was in our friendship, I wasn't even sure what changes I'd ask her to make. Be . . . nicer? Stop being . . . you?

I was thirty-two years old at the time, which means I knew some things about the world (the difference between a lager and a stout, how to pay my electric bill online), but I was still unsure of how to handle a substandard friend. Should I ghost her? Have a loud drunken fight at my birthday party? Tell everyone in my life about how wretched she was as a best friend but continue to hang out with her indefinitely? I chose the latter option, which isn't great. 0/10, would not recommend.

Our soft partnership hardened into a dictatorship. I started to fantasize that Brielle would find another friend and vanish. Perhaps she'd fall in love with one of her lanky fuckos and follow the fella to London or Vancouver or Shanghai—any scenario where I didn't have to confront her about wanting to end our friendship.

She made me feel like someone I didn't want to be. That was unacceptable and, ultimately, what made our friendship untenable. Our slow car crash of a friendship showed me that this whole friendship thing was much more complicated than I'd bargained for.

Juanita's Experience

Juanita's relationship with her boyfriend hit a snag, to put it mildly. She had discovered he'd cheated on her. As hurt as she was, she resisted telling her friends about what he'd done. Regardless, her friends picked up on the fact that something was off with her, which resulted in her friends—some of which she'd had for fifteen years—withdrawing.

Her friends pressed her for details. Her best friend told her, "If you can't be honest with me, good, bad, or ugly, then I need to take a step back from this friendship."

That broke Juanita's heart. She cried for months. This situation forced her to look inward and realize that her inability to be real with her friends created a chasm. Juanita had conflicting priorities: she wanted to protect her romantic relationship with her boyfriend, but she wanted to manage her friends' reactions too.

She finally divulged her troubles to her best friend. The experience made her realize she had deep-rooted people-pleasing tendencies that prevented her from being vulnerable. She was so busy trying to appease everyone around her that she assumed her friends couldn't handle the information about the infidelity.

"Protecting myself wasn't worth losing my friend," she said. "It was devastating. And it really forced me to open up." She's since made a commitment to herself to let her best friend know if there's anything distressing going on in her life. That's what close friends are for.

In Juanita's case, by not disclosing what was really going on to her friend, she created distance between them. To her friend, it felt like a form of lying by omission. Thankfully, Juanita was able to right the ship and maintain these relationships.

In my situation, Brielle hadn't lied to me or disclosed my secrets to anyone. There wasn't an event I could pinpoint that made me want to step away. Instead, all I felt was a gloomy atmosphere between us rather than true connection.

Dr. Glasser, the Choice Theory guy, identified **seven caring habits that lead to connection**,[1] which are all present in some capacity in a healthy friendship and exemplify emotional maturity.

1. Supporting

2. Encouraging

3. Listening

4. Accepting

5. Trusting

6. Respecting

7. Negotiating differences

While Brielle initially exhibited these traits, they fell away one by one, resulting in our disconnection. Most of these traits are self-evident. But the "negotiating differences" piece is more nuanced, as all of these can be either spoken or unspoken. John Gottman outlined a few of these friendship negotiations in his book *The Relationship Cure*:[2]

- How close and intimate will the friendship be?
- Will you share your true feelings with each other?
- How much time will you spend together?
- How will you maintain contact?
- Who will take the lead in scheduling plans?
- Who will play more of a support role?

The goal of these negotiations is to find balance and footing in the relationship so resentment is less likely to occur.

Dr. Glasser also identified **seven deadly disconnecting habits** that push people away:[3]

1. Complaining
2. Criticizing
3. Blaming
4. Nagging
5. Threatening
6. Punishing
7. Bribing or rewarding to control

Now I see that, over time, Brielle ticked more of the disconnection boxes than the connection ones. Is it any wonder that I felt the need to pull the plug on our friendship?

Misha's Experience

"I wish I knew how to broach difficulties or tension I'm having with certain friends," Misha told me. "It's really only a few friends, but it's often the same few. I always let it go and pretend like there's no issue, even when there is." Misha knows a handful of people who have successfully had productive talks with their friends where they come to a greater understanding. "But, I'm scared of saying the wrong thing, changing the chemistry, and coming off as petty or needy," she said.

Jillian's Experience

Jillian asked me why it's so taboo to end a friendship that's past its prime. If she had her druthers (my word, not hers), we'd normalize severing a friendship.

"There is incredible pressure to put up with shitty friends or friends who don't align with who you are," she said. She feels like it shouldn't be so stigmatized: "People change, and I think it's okay to end friendships." She's been surprised to learn that people tend not to agree with her on this. They get offended at the suggestion of cutting bait. "I've been met with so much resistance from friends who desperately want to try to make it work. But I don't want them to change, and I'm not going to change," she said. "Isn't it okay to just walk away with no hard feelings?"

Even on the subject of conflict, we see a range of opinions. On one hand, we have Misha, who does want to address conflicts but doesn't know how. On the other, we have Jillian, who just wants friendship breakups to be more accepted. Why do we have this attitude that friendships must persist forever when it's clear that that's an unreasonable expectation?

Kathleen's Experience

Kathleen has one friendship she considers a four out of ten in closeness. "We've known each other since elementary school, and despite seeing each other once a month to catch up, I frequently feel disconnected and have been mistreated by this friend. So that's a complex recurring issue, whether or not to keep this nearly lifelong friend in my life." She told me she struggles with severing the friendship, even though it's not ideal. They've been in each other's lives for so long, and it's scary for Kathleen to consider ending things.

WHY WE STAY IN UNHAPPY FRIENDSHIPS

There are five main reasons why someone might have trouble distancing themselves from a friendship that's no longer functional, according to *Psychology Today*.[4] Of course, it's possible to have more than one of these factors going on at once:

- **Long-standing ties.** There's lots of shared history between you two. This is Kathleen's issue.

- **Strong sense of loyalty.** The friend stood by your side during a challenging time or event, so it seems cruel to discard them from your life when you're doing better.

- **Reluctance to disrupt one's social life.** When you share a common social network, it can be very hard to remove yourself from the group because you're unhappy with one person in your crew. It's easier to just ignore your discomfort rather than risk being ousted from the social group.

- **Fear of potential conflict.** Negotiating new boundaries can be hard and downright scary. Sometimes it feels easier to resign yourself to the ill-fitting dynamic with a friend and keep the status quo. This is Misha's issue.

- **Straight-up ignorance.** Perhaps nobody taught you how to break up with a friend. You have no clue how to extricate yourself from a difficult situation like this.

Logically, I knew ending the friendship with Brielle would make my social life harder in the short term, but emotionally, the loyalty I had to her, my fear of conflict, and my ignorance of how to handle the situation swirled together into a rancid ball of shit.

Now that I know all of this, I can see that the main problems with walking away from Brielle were that we shared a social circle, I was afraid of fighting with her, and I had no clue how to navigate a friendship breakup. It was a perfect recipe for a miserable time.

Looking back, I knew my friendship with Brielle was in trouble, but I didn't understand *why* our friendship buckled. Now, knowing about why friendships either thrive or decay, my ambivalence makes perfect sense. Her bullying and entitlement impacted my willingness to continue our friendship. But it was my unwillingness to assert my boundaries that ultimately doomed the relationship. I didn't have the language, the where-withal, or the fortitude to take a hard look at myself. It was easier to keep the spotlight on Brielle's bad behavior than on my weak boundaries.

"When you have a long history of not telling someone what you want from them, you lose your feeling for them. You stop caring because caring means feeling powerless," Heather Havrilesky wrote in her "Ask Polly" column in *The Cut* in response to a woman who needed guidance on how to end a toxic friendship.[5]

Sure, the letter writer's roommate/friend was an obnoxious a-hole who exhibited all sorts of destructive, entitled behaviors. "But you won't know if she's still worth it until you speak up, without anger, and state what you need and what you won't do for her," Havrilesky wrote. "She will probably still be insecure and bitchy and threatened and a million other annoying things, but she might also learn a lot from the way you stood up for yourself and your needs without making it about what's wrong with her."

Lisa's Experience

Lisa told me that when she spends time with her high school friends—whom she's lived apart from for over a decade—she sometimes finds herself slipping into old patterns. "These include allowing my boundaries to be transgressed, staying quiet about my needs to avoid conflict, and other things I've worked hard to improve," she told me. She moved to Philly from Boston in the fall of 2020, so it's hard for her to separate the pandemic from the move in terms of effects on her friendships.

"I will say it made making new friends in a new city difficult and slow. On the other hand, I think there's been a cultural shift in the way we talk about the human need for connection and the punishing pain of isolation and loneliness. In my experience there's a lot less shame and stigma associated with being lonely. It's more acceptable and easier to 'need' other people in order to be okay. This has made it easier for me to deepen the friendships I did start once things started opening back up."

Friendships are not mysterious, untamable, unknowable experiences that passively happen to us; they are relationships we actively choose to invest time, care, and attention in. These are relationships we elect to grow within.

Rebecca's Experience

I asked Rebecca what she wished she would've known about friendships as a young person. Would it have helped if she was more prepared for how difficult managing friendships in adulthood would be? "Honestly, I don't wish I would have known anything about adult friendships as a child, as I think it would have made me sad," she said.

"What I would have liked to have known earlier was that sometimes you need to have hard conversations and it's worth it. We have them in romantic relationships; why not have them in friendships?" She still struggles with letting go of her older bonds. "I still have a lot of feelings about the fact that my best friends from high school are no longer my best friends," she said. "I always wonder if having hard conversations could have helped to save them."

If you're struggling with ironing out wrinkles in your long-held friendships, please have self-compassion. You're not alone. Lots of us (myself included, obviously) have struggled with knowing what to do or say to leave a friendship.

Ultimately, with Brielle, she disclosed one of my secrets to a mutual friend, and that's when I knew I was done fighting for our friendship. When I found out she'd spilled the beans, I confronted her. She apologized for breaking my trust, but it wasn't enough. I told her that it was best we go our separate ways. I was direct and firm. We haven't spoken since.

HOW TO TAKE A STEP BACK FROM NON-TOXIC FRIENDSHIPS WITHOUT FEELING LIKE AN INSENSITIVE DEMON

Sometimes we don't want to pursue friendships with very nice people. It can feel awkward to constantly turn a friend down, especially one so eager to be in your life. How do you decline their invitations without coming off like a jerk or making up excuses? The key is to be gracious, direct, and warm, in that order.

"Thank you for reaching out [gracious], but I'm not interested in joining a mead tasting club [direct]. Best of luck getting a crew of mead enthusiasts together [warm]."

"Thanks for the lunch invite [gracious], but I like to use my lunch breaks to catch up on my reading [direct]. Happy eating! [warm]."

"Thanks for dropping a line [gracious], but my schedule is quite full this month so I can't attend your barbecue [direct]. Enjoy the nice weather while it's here! [warm]."

If you feel like you need to send a stronger message that you no longer want to continue the friendship, full stop, then say that.

"Thank you for reaching out to schedule dinner [gracious]. I appreciate your effort, but I can't dedicate more time to our friendship at the moment [direct]. I wish you all the best [warm]."

This is a great strategy because if you change your mind at any point in the future, hopefully the door will still be open to connect.

....

Exercise: Map a Fallout with a Friend

Repeat this exercise for as many friendships as needed to gain clarity for any friendship breakups.

_____

Name of friend you had conflict with:

_____

Why you stayed in the friendship as long as you did:

☐ Long-standing tie

☐ Sense of loyalty

☐ Reluctance to disrupt your social life

☐ Fear of conflict

☐ Avoidance

How things ended:

☐ You ended the friendship

☐ Distanced yourself from the friend

☐ Compartmentalized aspects of the friendship

Reflection questions:

1. Is there anything you would have done differently to address the conflict with your friend?

    _____

2. What advice would you give to your younger self in this situation?

    _____

3. How does diagnosing this breakup make you feel?

    _____

....

The first step to understanding if a friendship can be salvaged is to know why the equilibrium has changed. Part 2 of this book is all about how to maintain this delicate balance so you never again have to wonder why a friendship is (or isn't) working, or figure out how to get it back on track if you find it's worth mending. In the next part, I'll explain exactly what a loving friendship needs in order to thrive and how to make those changes a reality.

PART 2

MATTERING TO OTHERS

10

Desire, Diligence, and Delight

Given all that we know about the challenges of modern friendship, how can we forge ahead? How can we apply everything we've learned about what motivates the development of friendships in our lives?

Guy Fieri had his triple Ds with his television show *Diners, Drive-Ins and Dives*. In this book, we'll focus on a different trio of Ds: Desire, Diligence, and Delight. These are the three crucial factors that account for happy, healthy, and fulfilling modern friendships.

Desire is the wish to spend time with a friend. Desire is saying, "I want to be friends with this particular person." Any platonic relationship starts—and ends—with the desire to be friends because friendships are voluntary.

Desire looks like:

- Willing to be in a friendship with a particular person or group
- Wishing to learn about the other person's world and share your own
- Knowing exactly why you are both in each other's lives
- Feeling motivated to stay in each other's lives

Just as your car won't make it to Trader Joe's without enough gas, your friendship car will not move forward without a sufficient amount of desire being present. Lack of desire looks like:

- Not answering texts or phone calls
- Declining plans
- Feeling like hanging out with this person will not be a good use of your time
- Feeling indifferent to whether the friendship continues or not
- Feeling drained at the thought of connecting with this person

Desire is subjective and exists on a spectrum. Of course, as we've learned, sometimes a lack of desire to continue a friendship isn't anyone's fault. People can lose their desire to be in a friendship for all sorts of reasons at any time. Sometimes desire tapers off due to personal factors (you no longer enjoy the other person's company). Sometimes it's a matter of logistics (you don't live near each other or your availability has changed). If you're grieving, struggling, or going through a difficult time, friendships may not be your—or your friend's—top priority. That's completely understandable and expected. As much as we wish we could wave a wand and have it be different, desire can't be forced through sheer will. It doesn't work like that.

Diligence is prioritizing spending time with your friend. It's about being attentive to the important things going on in your friend's life. Noticing changes in their other relationships and family and work obligations. It's also about being attuned to their moods and interests.

Diligence is thinking, *I promise to show up for this person to the best of my ability when it truly matters. I will ask my friend to get together to do something we both enjoy, and we will make it happen.*

Again, consider car ownership. There are serious consequences when you ignore your duties as a car owner. If you neglect these (boring, adultish) commitments like having current registration, insurance, inspections, etc., you will get a ticket. Your car might even be impounded. Diligence in friendship is a lot like that: taking care of the details so your car is able to run properly.

The actions you take as a dear friend will make or break the strength of your bond. Diligence is the nitty-gritty shit. It's reaching out when your friend is drowning and letting them know that you're there for them. It's the act of honoring the commitment you've made to each other as friends. Diligence looks like:

- Remembering important events in your friends' lives (births, deaths, anniversaries, etc.)
- Being accountable and owning decisions you make as their friend
- Being authentic with your availability and needs
- Making appropriate gestures when milestone events occur
- Inviting your friends to get together in a way that takes their other commitments into account
- Being mindful of limitations your friends may have (financial, physical, emotional, etc.)
- Actually checking out the podcast, movie, or TV show your friends recommend to you

Lack of diligence is why friendships often fade à la the family picture in *Back to the Future*. Diligence gives structure to the friendship. It constructs a house for the friendship to live in. Lack of diligence is a lot like letting that foundation for the friendship rot, and it could look like:

- Being flaky or ghosting on plans made
- Canceling plans and never offering to reschedule
- Not celebrating personal milestones
- Ignoring important professional accomplishments
- Going long periods of time without communication
- Never engaging with your friend's recommendations

If there is a lack of diligence in a close friendship, then the relationship will feel superficial, as you won't feel truly supported in the totality of your life. This could be the work friend who is great for sharing a turkey wrap and office gossip but isn't emotionally available when you're going through a heartbreaking divorce. Or the wild friend who makes you pop a button laughing but doesn't reply to your text asking if she's free on Friday night to grab dinner. The diligence portion of a friendship lets your friends know that their well-being *matters* to you. It's putting thought into action.

Delight is the support and reciprocity each friend offers the other. It's about enjoying the time you spend together. Delight is thinking, *This friendship is a perfect fit for me.* It's using your words, thoughts, and actions to make both people in the relationship feel nourished, accepted, and respected.

I swear, this is the last time I'll use a car metaphor in this book, but in automotive terms, delight is the reason why your car feels like it's *your* car that's perfect for *your* needs. For example, I drive a zippy red Jetta because I'm a middle-aged woman who uses acid toners and listens to Taylor Swift. I would not enjoy driving a Lamborghini or Mack truck to pick up a Greek salad at Whole Foods. Those vehicles (too flashy, too unwieldy) don't make sense for my needs or lifestyle.

Just as people aren't a monolith who all want to drive the same make and model of car, the friendships we choose are tailored to our specific tastes. We all have highly individualized reasons for the cars (or bikes, motorcycles, scooters, etc.) we choose because we have particular needs for our transportation. Friendships are the same.

Delight in a friendship looks like:

- Being vulnerable in sharing your lives with one another

- Having friends give you the benefit of the doubt and assume you always act with the best of intentions

- Forgiving each other for the times when you were still learning how to get this close friendship thing right

Delight is also about what you refrain from doing as much as it's about what you choose to do. Dishing out unsolicited advice or acting like you know your friend's life better than they do doesn't make you a great friend to be around. It's about approaching your friend as a compassionate teammate, not as a domineering pseudo-boss.

If there is no delight, then the friendship will feel draining, constricting, suffocating. You might resent having to show up for your friend's tough times without the relief of delightful camaraderie. You may feel criticized or bullied by this person. Cowed. Smaller.

Once delight in a friendship evaporates, desire for the friendship will also plummet. You may not be able to put your disinterest into words, but your actions will show it. Your diligence in attending to the friendship will lower out of apathy. Soon you'll be left with a husk of a friendship.

A big component of delight is how well your friends understand the various roles you play in your own life. Psychologist and author of *Platonic: How the Science of Attachment Can Help You Make—and Keep—Friends*, Marisa Franco, calls this "identity affirmation."

"Your friend will affirm an identity for you that they might not have for themselves," she told me in an interview.[1] "Maybe your friend's really artsy and wants to go quit their job and do an artist's retreat. And if you don't have good identity support or affirmation, they'll just be like, 'What do you mean? You're not going to get paid? Why would you quit your job?' You would impose all of your judgments and values onto them." This is concerning because you could potentially be leading them down the wrong path. "They're not going to be happy if they live life according to what you want," she said. "They're only going to be happy if they live life according to what they want."

People who are good at offering identity affirmation are able to say, "My friend is living according to their values. Even if those aren't my values, I can still support them on their own individual, authentic path."

Friends who encourage our self-actualization, who encourage our truest self, bring a lot of safety, security, and depth to the friendship, Dr. Franco said.

These three elements of desire, delight, and diligence provide the foundation for any functional, enjoyable friendship. They make a friendship s'more: chocolatey smooth desire, melting with the sweet, gooey marshmallow of delight, all contained within a solid foundation of a diligent graham cracker.

Is your friendship doomed if you don't have all three Ds present in equal numbers? Not necessarily. As long as you have a desire to be friends with someone, there will always be a possibility of connection, just like if there's gas in your car, you can theoretically move forward. But the likelihood of maintaining a nourishing connection depends on the quality of the other two Ds.

There's always hope for friendships to find sturdier ground if both friends have the desire to stay in the friendship. But to enjoy that life-affirming, snuggly legging friendship where you'd give an enthusiastic speech extolling what your friendship means to you both, you need the three Ds.

Yes, our friendships can be difficult and confusing. But you can take control and re-engineer your friendships to be a better fit for your busy life today. And that's exactly what this part of the book will walk you through: how to encourage desire, practice diligence, and increase delight in your friendships. This will allow the people you love to feel the affection you have for them for a long, long time. I'll teach you how to put all this knowledge into practice by modulating the words you say, the actions you do, and the thoughts you think toward your cherished friends.

Since writing this book, I've noticed changes in how I approach my loved ones:

- I'm more willing to examine my feelings before I react to them.

- I'm more flexible and give my friends the benefit of the doubt.

- I'm better able to combat the insecure voice in my head that panics when my expectations aren't met.

- I'm more aware of the choices I make and what emotional and psychological tools are in my toolbox.

- I voice my appreciation a lot more. I tell my friends I love them. I give them permission to hang back if they need it, and I assure them I'm not going anywhere.

You will see these changes too! As we transition to a more hands-on approach, here's how you can prepare:

Give yourself time and space to complete the exercises. Stash your phone away. Keep a pen or pencil handy. Give yourself permission to reflect on the questions I ask. There's no rush here. Take your time.

Cultivate chill vibes. Wear loose-fitting clothes. Take your bra off if you're wearing one and it's appropriate for you to do so. Wear fluffy socks. Settle in somewhere comfy. Light a favorite candle. Play soft music in the background. Personally, I like playing video game soundtracks or a lo-fi beats playlist when I need to concentrate.

Have a willingness to dig deep. A variety of emotions might bubble up when you approach these exercises. Not all memories may be happy ones you're eager to revisit: anger at a friend who let you down, pain at a friend who abandoned you, shame that you mishandled a sensitive situation, sadness at a friend who slipped out of your life and you're still unsure why they made that choice. It's A LOT. Take breaks, and if you need to step away and come back, totally do that.

Be patient. Meaningful change in the way you engage with your friends will take time. Be patient with yourself as you undergo this process. Be gentle with yourself if raw or embarrassing memories emerge. You're evolving here. In travel terms, becoming a wholehearted friend is a cross-country road trip, not a quick trip to Jamba Juice. Every day is an opportunity to apply what you've learned.

11

The Secret to Getting a Hell Yes! Every Time

I n 2001, I worked as a circulation manager at a small fashion magazine based in Tribeca. As part of my job, I arranged a promotion to offer free copies of our magazine to Urban Outfitters customers. I even took the train from Penn Station in New York to 30th Street Station in Philly to meet with the Urban Outfitters' rep to set the whole thing up. That was my first-ever business trip, and I felt very adult with my nice pants and professional-looking black leather purse.

But my days of taking business trips didn't last long. In 2002, after getting laid off in the immediate wake of 9/11, I moved twenty minutes outside of Philly. Because I was unemployed and new in town, I reached out to my contact at Urban Outfitters to let him know I was looking for a job. *Urban Outfitters is a large company. There must be something I can do for them*, I thought. *Maybe I can write a blog for their website? Or write copy for their catalog?* I was open to anything! He passed my résumé on to human resources like a *mensch*.

Fortunately, a lady from human resources called me in for an interview with the head of the department, a woman named Lonnie. Well, a job interview necessitated a job interview outfit. I raced to H&M at the Cherry Hill Mall that afternoon and picked out a sharp-looking fitted red sweater. I think I'd read in a women's magazine that wearing red is a sign of strength, so I wanted to channel some of that ferocious "hire me" energy.

On interview day, I paired the sweater with a denim skirt one could describe as lightly rock 'n' roll. There was a white guitar screen printed over the bottom half of the skirt that looked incredibly cool, trust me.

I came in for the interview with my battle-ready red sweater and guitar skirt, and waited for my name to be called.

"Anna? Lonnie's ready for you," the woman at the front desk said. "Right this way."

She ushered me into a large office with exposed brick walls and furniture made of reclaimed wood. Lonnie—perky, blonde, petite—stood up and shook my hand.

"Welcome! I looked over your résumé. It was interesting. I figured we should meet. Unfortunately," she said with a frown, "I don't have any positions open for you at the moment."

"Okaaaay," I said, trying to hide the "WTF?!" expression on my face. I came all the way down and purchased new clothes for nothing. There wasn't a job for me. She just wanted to see what my vibe was. That was great, I suppose, but I wasn't any closer to paying my bills. I felt swindled, like she'd wasted my time. We were two women in nice-ish clothes who were talking about a job that didn't exist.

"I will keep your information on file," she added. "If anything comes up, I'll reach out. I'm so happy we met!"

Fledgling friendships can fall into this trap too. Sometimes, like my non-job interview with Lonnie, a reason for getting together with a promising new friend is as flimsy as, "You seem interesting." We've all done it. We think we should reach out to the spunky girl in our apartment building. We should invite the new coworker with purple-streaked hair to lunch. We should set up a coffee date with the engaging woman we keep seeing at the gym. But once we're in the same room with our iced coffee cups leaving water rings on the café table and our respective harvest grain bowls in front of our faces, we discover we have no clue what to talk about.

Sure, you can start with the standards:

- Tell me about yourself.

- What do you do?

- Where do you like to hang out?

- Where did you grow up?

- Do you have siblings?

- Are you married? What does your spouse do?

- Any pets? Cats? Dogs?

At the end of the hangout, once the plates are cleared, you might have a flash of a thought: *She seems nice, but* this (finding the time to get together, settling on a place to go, having to come up with things to talk about) *felt like too much work. Why do I feel like something's missing? What's wrong with me?*

You might even tell this promising new friend, "We should do this again!" but you know deep down that your heart's not in it. This new-comer friendship probably isn't going anywhere, and you're not sure why.

To that I'd say you probably made the same mistake the HR lady made with me: we didn't identify a clear and compelling reason we should get together. Lonnie didn't tell me: "I want to interview you for a blogger position we have open." She didn't have any idea what slot she'd fit me into before we met. That was the problem. We tried to figure it out on the spot, which was a risk that didn't work.

Betty's Experience

Both Betty and her good friend Jill have daughters on the cusp of turning one. Betty wishes she connected more with Jill. "I guess it's no one's fault," Betty told me. "We'll text back and forth here and there. Share pictures of the babies. Once, Jill was like, 'Would you want to FaceTime with the girls sometime?' And I was like, 'Yeah, sure. Totally.'"

But a meeting never made it to the calendar. The thought "We should get together!" hangs in the air and evaporates. Betty, reflecting on this exchange, seems resigned. Unless one of the friends initiates, those hangouts never happen. They just become a wish or dream.

In 2011, Adam Teterus popped into Fat Jack's Comicrypt to see what new comic books were available. He settled on the premiere issue of *Spider-Man: Miles Morales*. Then he returned to work helping customers at the Apple Store in downtown Philly.

When one purchases an individual issue of a comic book—aka floppies—the cashier slips it into a distinctive thin brown paper bag. In the break room in the Apple Store basement, Adam slapped the bag down on the table and wolfed down his lunch.

"Oh, you like comics?" his coworker Octavius said, nodding toward the slim brown bag.

Adam had no idea Octavius, a recently married, churchgoing man in his thirties, was a fellow comic book fan. They immediately bonded over their shared love of The Avengers, Wonder Woman, Batman, and all the rest. It wasn't long before they figured other people might get a kick out of their discussions too, so they started a podcast where they mused over news and events taking place in the comics universe.

One day during the summer of 2016, Octavius arrived to record an episode of their podcast. Adam could tell immediately that something was off. Octavius seemed sluggish.

Octavius, or Ock, as Adam calls him, shared that he'd recently been diagnosed with stage four kidney failure. "I knew he was upset, obviously," Adam said. "I knew he was unwell. But I didn't know anything else. I don't know what kidneys do. I don't know anything about this situation."[1]

Ock needed to find a living donor among his friends and family, but it couldn't be just anyone: he needed a donation from somebody who matched his specific blood type, O positive.[2]

"I'm O positive," Adam said in disbelief. Even though it's a match, Ock didn't want to get his hopes up. He'd already had two O positive potential donors, his wife and mother, but both were ruled out as donors. Just being the same blood type wasn't enough. Adam would have to endure rigorous tests to make sure his kidney was a viable match to his friend.

Adam didn't hesitate to jump into action. He set up a slew of medical appointments to determine if he was a viable candidate, and miraculously, Adam's kidney was indeed a perfect match for his friend.

The operation took place in October 2016. "[The transplant] changed a lot about us," Adam told me.[3] "But also," he marveled, "nothing has changed." The anniversary of the transplant, October 11, comes and goes without any fanfare. "We just forget about it," Adam said, laughing. "How can you forget about something so monumental? It's funny the way that it's beside the point."

"I don't know how—or if—we would have ever been close to one another if we didn't have that one little thing that became a keyhole into each other's lives. And then that one little thing widened," Adam said, "and we just trust each other."

Two months after the transplant, Ock told Adam he was going to be a father. He asked if Adam would be his daughter's godfather. Now they're more than friends; they're family. In fact, their families spend Christmas together. Adam and Ock's experience demonstrates the power of a shared passion. All this—a lifesaving operation, a chosen family, an unbreakable bond—was generated from a brown paper comic book bag on a lunch table.

Yes, this story shows the incredible result of a strong friendship, but it also illustrates the power of a compelling *about* in a friendship. In the case of Ock and Adam, they were clear about their shared interests, which provided the foundation for a strong relationship. Along these lines, Dr. Dunbar identified seven pillars of friendship in his book *Friends: Understanding the Power of our Most Important Relationships*:[4]

- Speaking the same language
- Growing up in the same location
- Having the same educational and career experiences

- Enjoying the same hobbies and interests

- Sharing the same worldview (morals, religious views, political leanings)

- Having similar senses of humor

- Sharing the same musical tastes

Looking at Adam and Ock's friendship, their love of comic books was the portal, the seed, that allowed their friendship to grow into something incredible.

"Friendship must be about something even if it were only an enthusiasm for dominoes or white mice," C. S. Lewis wrote in his book *The Four Loves*. "Those who have nothing can share nothing; those who are going nowhere can have no fellow travelers."[5]

If you're feeling a friendship start to wane, the reason to be in the friendship might be unclear or outdated. This is a problem because every close friendship needs a reason for both people to pursue it wholeheartedly.

Lucy's Experience

Lucy was good friends with her roommate, Emily. They used to hit the town together and have oodles of midtwenties girl fun. Then, Emily moved away, and both women partnered with significant others. Lucy now has a child.

In a tale as old as time, their friendship floundered. "We have different lives," Lucy told me. "I don't know if the about is there anymore with her because I honestly don't talk to her that much anymore. And when I do, I'll text her, and it's like, 'Hey, how you doing?' And that's it. There's just not much to say."

"I feel guilty," Lucy said, furrowing her brow. "I wish I had something to ask her, but I don't."

Sasha's Experience

Sasha has a hard time with friends' noncommitment. "It's been hard to accept the Seattle attitude that it's okay to 'not have the bandwidth' to hang out or celebrate a friend's events," Sasha tells me. "If someone feels like canceling an hour before you were going to get together, they will." She feels like her friends from earlier days honored their commitments more. "I don't think it's just that life is more complicated as an adult," she said. She thinks people feel emboldened, like bailing has become more socially acceptable.

People, generally speaking, don't bail on plans when there's a clear and compelling reason to show up. If your boss asks you to lunch to talk about your future at your job, you're going to be at the meeting. When the bank calls and says there's a problem with your account, you return the call or pop into a branch to untangle the situation. It's easier to make time to show up for something if you're clear on the reason for it.

Whereas if a friend says, "Hey, let's grab drinks!" and you don't know why you're getting together other than to knock back a few glasses of Shiraz, you're more likely to feel like the hangout isn't a priority. Hence, the bailing, flaking, and cancelling.

C. S. Lewis said the biggest mistake people make when looking for friends is that they don't focus on the reason both individuals should want to be in the friendship.[6] As you embark on forging new friendships or trying to reignite old ones, ask yourself: Do we have a clear and compelling reason to seek each other out? What can we do together that will incite passion and irresistible excitement? The reason has to be so compelling, meaningful, and enjoyable that both people will carve out time in their life to connect over it.

I'm a writer, and a lot of my friends are writers too. So I'll often reach out to a local writer I admire and say, "Hey! I love your work. Would you want to get together and work on writing sometime? We can meet at your favorite café." Here, my reason for reaching out is clear, and specific: I am extending an invitation to write together. From there, the recipient can decide if the clear reason I gave is compelling enough for them to accept my offer. Of course, if this person is taking a step back from writing or already has enough writing partners, they might turn me down. In this case, my invitation wasn't compelling enough to them *at this time*.

With new friends, by frontloading the effort in the invitation, you won't have to work so hard to find something to talk about once you're in the same room. Look at the difference between these invitations.

A STRANGER

Invitation #1: "Hey! I'm new in town. Would you like to meet up for coffee?"

Invitation #2: "Hey! I'm <u>new in town</u>. I saw that we have kids in the same school. Would you like to <u>meet up for coffee so I can hear all about your experience living in the community</u>?"

What do I want? to meet up for coffee to hear about their experiences.

Why? Because I'm new in town.

Is this compelling enough for the person to say yes? Maybe. If they're lonely and looking for new friends, this could be compelling.

AN ACQUAINTANCE

Invitation #1: "Hey! I've been thinking about you. Would you like to grab lunch sometime?"

Invitation #2: "Hey! I saw on LinkedIn that you left your job. That's so brave. I want to <u>hear all about how you came to the decision and what your next steps are</u>. Maybe I can help in some way! Would you like to <u>grab lunch this week</u>?"

What do I want? To grab lunch.

Why? To discuss her job situation and see if I can help.

Is this compelling enough for the person to say yes? Sure, especially if you are in a position to help.

Exercise

Now you try crafting clear and compelling invitations.

For a friend you've lost touch with

Invitation #1: "I've missed hanging out with you. Are you around to hop on a call in the next week or so and catch up?"

Invitation #2: "I've missed hanging out with you. I saw on social media that you recently got divorced. I don't know if you knew this, but I'm divorced too. It can feel really lonely. Are you around to hop on a call in the next week or so? I want to hear all about how you're navigating everything."

Underline the clear and compelling reasons I offered in Invitation #2.

What do I want?

_____

Why?

_____

Is this compelling enough for the person to say yes?

_____

For a close friend

Invitation #1: "Happy birthday, darling. When can we celebrate?"

Invitation #2: "Happy birthday, darling. I want to hear all about what you've been working on and see if we can plan a girls' trip for us later in the year. When can we celebrate? Does Tuesday night work for you?"

Underline the clear and compelling reasons I offered in Invitation #2.

What do I want?

_____

Why?

_____

Is this compelling enough for the person to say yes?

_____

I hope these examples illustrate how important it is to properly frame invitations to friends—new, old, and everything in between. If you give a clear, compelling reason to connect, you will find more success in your connection efforts.

When you're in a committed relationship, giving your friend a clear, compelling reason to get together makes it easier for them to prioritize your hangout by organizing childcare, negotiating with their partner, or rearranging their commitments and obligations. This way your friend can make the case that spending time with you is important.

Desire to stay in a friendship isn't a mystery. We all yearn for a friend because of specific, highly personal reasons. When you say you want friends, you probably don't mean just anyone in the universe. You probably don't mean the mail carrier or the random person next to you on the bus. No, you mean you are looking to be with a friend who marvels at the world in the specific way you do, who laughs at the same shit you laugh at.

There's always a reason why you're attracted to some people and not attracted to others. Using what we learned in Choice Theory, we can understand how we can choose others and who chooses us.

Charlie's Experience

"My biggest issue with friendships in adulthood is my own opinion of myself," Charlie told me. "I often feel boring and uninteresting, and so I end up feeling like people will only want to be in friendship with me if I am giving more than I'm getting. But that imbalance doesn't lead to robust, enduring friendships," he said. "It's something I'm working on."

It made me sad when Charlie shared this with me. I reminded him that friendships start by bonding over a passion or hobby and encouraged him to find something he loves to do and find people who love doing that thing too. Lots of people want drama-free friends who are good listeners and are trustworthy and reliable. There's a lot you can offer people, even if you aren't the life of the party.

Exercise: Brainstorm Activities You Can Do with Friends

Instead of simply thinking, *I wish I had a friend*, finish the wish by adding an activity you'd like to do with them.

- "I'd like a friend to go see comedy shows with."
- "I'd like a friend to go on Disney cruises with."
- "I'd like a friend to eat Korean food with."
- "I'd like a friend to learn surfing with."

Now it's your turn:

I want a friend to go (place) _____ with.

I want a friend to go (place) _____ with.

I want a friend to go (place) _____ with.

I want a friend to do (recreational activity) _____ with.

I want a friend to do (recreational activity) _____ with.

I want a friend to do (recreational activity) _____ with.

I want a friend to do (recreational activity) _____ with.

If you want to understand why you gravitate toward some friends and not others, it's usually because friendships revolving around *something* have a steadier foundation. They have a built-in reason why both people yearn to spend time with one another.

Some friendships are about drinking Vodka Red Bulls and dancing at the club until the houselights flicker on. Some friendships are about sharing the struggles of raising kids. Other friendships are about being from the same town or school. And some are about horse racing, laser tag, or running marathons.

Friendships can be built on any interest, like those nerdy kids who play *Dungeons & Dragons* in someone's basement once a week. They're onto something! They've identified a concrete reason to get together: to talk about ogres and eat Cool Ranch Doritos, I imagine.

I have an entire friendship with a woman named Sari because we both love the band Fall Out Boy. I met her on Twitter, and we've met up at various Fall Out Boy concerts over the past decade. As it turns out, Sari and I were onto something too. Music is a fantastic thing to bond over. In fact, music tastes are one of Dr. Dunbar's seven pillars of friendships.

"The more of these boxes you tick with someone, the more time you will be prepared to invest in them, the more emotionally close you will feel towards them, the closer they will lie to you in the layers of your social network, and the more willing you will be to help them out when they need it," Dr. Dunbar wrote.[7] "And the more likely they are to help you."

Speaking the same language or growing up in the same location may not be a compelling enough reason when two people live in the same U.S. city, but if you're an expat living in Mongolia, who knows? Maybe having an English-speaking friend from your hometown *is* enough of a reason to pursue a friendship. You don't even have to go all the way to Mongolia. Maybe if you live on the East Coast and move to the West Coast, you'll find companionship with other people who made that move too.

The more pillars you have in common with your friends, the more likely you will have reasons to continue your connection. The *about* is the reason you both make time to pursue the friendship. It will help if you can articulate what a particular friendship in your life is about:

- Having children who attend the same school
- Playing online video games together
- Going to see Academy Award–winning movies
- Eating roasted turkey legs at Renaissance fairs
- Geeking out over skin care products
- Gossiping about Bravo's *Real Housewives* shows
- Trying new restaurants in town
- Working out
- Being a book nerd
- Attending the same college
- Grieving similar losses like losing a parent
- Being newly divorced or newly married
- Learning to speak Mandarin
- Being interested in clothes and fashion
- Sharing the same coworking space
- Having an interest in home-brewing beer

The abouts of a friendship can (and will) change. It's not a big problem as long as everyone in the friendship grows together in the same direction. The friendship that started with frequenting emo concerts could transform into being about having children in kindergarten or volunteering for political campaigns or whatever.

We can't force a friendship to happen any more than we can force a cat to get a black belt in karate. But there *must* be some reason friends continue to seek each other out. There *must* be a reason why the friendship persists. When the reason is unclear, the friendship will become less of a priority for one or both people.

As we learned in chapter 4, all behavior is informed by our inherent, genetic desires for survival, love and belonging, power, freedom, and fun.

How we go about fulfilling those needs is how we achieve the Quality Pictures we have in our Quality Worlds. The desire to pursue and maintain a friendship with another person is shaped by these competing—and sometimes contradictory—drives.

For instance, suppose I have a lovely new boss. Let's call her Selina. Sure, it'd be fun to let loose and knock back a few Coronas together after work one day. I could crack her up with some hilarious stories about my more unsavory exes, but I also want Selina to see me as a capable, dedicated employee. In fact, I'd really like her to consider me for a promotion in the coming months. In this case, my desire for a potential promotion (power) supersedes my desire to go out with her for some rowdy drinks (fun).

We make decisions by weighing out our needs all the time.

- You want to adopt a puppy (love and belonging, fun), but you don't because your landlord won't allow tenants to have pets in the apartment (survival).

- You consider applying for the perfect job across the country (power), but you hesitate because your significant other can't move with you (love and belonging).

- You want to quit your job (freedom), but you stay in the role because you have bills to pay (survival).

- You want to go back to school to take some classes in hopes of getting a better job (power, survival), but that would mean having less time to see friends and family (love and belonging).

When it comes to spending our time with friends, we make the same calculations on a subconscious level. The solution is to gain clarity on what your friendship is about.

Ultimately, nothing came of my meeting with Lonnie. I never got the job at Urban Outfitters, as she never figured out what role I could play. But I did learn that I won't buy a new item of clothing until I know for sure why my presence is required at an event.

Exercise: Take a "What's It About" Inventory

Identify what your friendships are about. Trace the evolution of your friendships by listing as many abouts as you can.

Friend #1

Name:

_____

Past about(s) in the friendship:

_____

Present about(s) in the friendship:

_____

Potential future about(s) in the friendship:

_____

Friend #2

Name:

_____

Past about(s) in the friendship:

_____

Present about(s) in the friendship:

_____

Potential future about(s) in the friendship:

_____

Friend #3

Name:

_____

Past about(s) in the friendship:

_____

Present about(s) in the friendship:

_____

Potential future about(s) in the friendship:

_____

WHEN THE ABOUT OF THE FRIENDSHIP IS UNCLEAR

Option #1: Recruit an accountability buddy to meet a goal.

Sometimes we have a friend from a distant but important part of our life: the old neighborhood, school, etc. You might have incredible affection toward this person but no clear reason why you should stay in touch, other than the past. One strategy is to see if you two can join forces to achieve an important goal for you both. Be each other's accountability buddy.

Psychology professor Gail Matthews wanted to learn about how goals are achieved, so in 2007, she conducted a study involving 267 participants from a wide swath of professional backgrounds in six countries between the ages of 23 and 72.[8] She identified four factors that contributed to the participants' goal completion:

- Writing down your clear goals
- Committing to achieving them
- Sharing the goal with a friend
- Sending weekly progress reports to this accountability buddy

Her research shows that accountability has a positive effect on goal outcomes. When incorporating all four steps, nearly three-quarters of the participants met their goal. That's how powerful sharing your goals with a friend can be!

A sample goal for you could look like: I'd like to move my body more, or I'd like to learn Italian. Once you commit to your goal, notify a dear friend who might share the goal: "I'd like to move my body more. Want to join me?" Then you can update each other weekly on your move report.

With this accountability system, not only will you be more likely to meet your goal of moving more, but you'll have a strong reason to maintain regular contact with each other. Here are some examples of how accountability buddies can propel us forward. Circle any that you'd be interested in starting with someone in your own social circle.

- **Fitness buddies.** Setting workout schedules, sharing meal plans, and regularly checking in with each other to ensure you're both sticking to your goals will lead to better results. Making a lifestyle change can be hard, and this kind of camaraderie can help positive changes stick.

- **Academic buddies.** Forming study groups, sharing resources, and helping explain difficult concepts to one another will keep everyone in the group focused and motivated. This kind of collaboration can lead to improved academic performance.

- **Career-minded buddies.** Colleagues can definitely help each other level up in their careers. Attending networking events, updating each other's résumé, and completing continuing education classes can help the partnership achieve desired career objectives.

- **Bad habit busting buddies.** If you're trying to quit smoking, gambling, online shopping, or some other undesirable habit, having someone to share your progress with can keep both people motivated and on track.

- **Creative buddies.** Artists, writers, musicians etc., can also benefit from this arrangement. Think of those famous writer salons and art collectives that nurtured pockets of talent throughout the ages. Having a tight-knit community of working artists allows creatives to share ideas, critique each other's work, and help lift one another up when creative slumps occur.

When picking an accountability buddy, make sure everyone in the arrangement is on the same page with enthusiasm, trust, style, and frequency of communication. It might even be worth it to talk about how to end the partnership at the appropriate time. Perhaps it's when a goal is met (when we've stopped smoking for three months) or after a period of time (when the school year ends). Everything is negotiable in these setups, so make sure you're comfortable with the time commitment.

Regular check-ins, honest feedback, and celebrating each other's achievements will create an effective partnership. Just in writing this book, I had accountability buddies at every step of the way, from working on the proposal, to writing the draft, and beyond. Each of these buddies brought their own talent, experience, and heart to helping me craft this book. And I hope my experience and heart helped them shape their projects too. Yay, accountability buddies!

Option #2: Propose suggestions for a new reason to get together.

"I'm learning how to paint watercolors. Do you want to learn how to paint with me?"

"I want to learn how to surf. Any interest in taking lessons with me?"

"I want to learn how to write poetry. Want to take a class with me?"

Having a strong *about* in your friendships will help both people understand *why* they are carving time to hang out. They can say, "I'm making time for my friend because . . ."

- We're in a walking group at the local mall.

- We're learning tarot card reading together.

- We're in a writing group.

- We're taking a spin class.

- We're on a trivia team together.

- We're recording a podcast about true crime.

- We love watching local theater together.

Option #3: Negotiate a new *about.*

Say you and your friend used to live together in your twenties. Now that you're coupled up and aren't able to spend unlimited hours watching movies and hanging out at local bars, your friendship has been feeling uncertain. It's time to negotiate your friendship's *about.* You could always nominate yourself to be your friend's accountability buddy:

- A friend from high school: "Tell me about your dreams. What would you like to learn or change, and how can I help as your friend?"

- A camp friend from childhood: "I have an idea: Will you be my travel buddy? Maybe we can take one big vacation every autumn. Thoughts?"

- A local acquaintance: "We met because our children are at the same school. I'm thinking of starting a hiking club. Would you want to do it with me?"

- A friend from work: "I want to get better at networking. Want to attend some local skill-building workshops with me?"

If you can't come up with a reason to continue the friendship, consider putting it on pause, and just let it be. Pretend it's taking a nap or it went on vacation to Palm Springs. Yes, you can still be friendly with one another. You can wish each other happy birthday and whatnot. But you might need to let the friendship hibernate until a clear and compelling reason emerges. Come back to the friendship later when you're in a different season of life.

If you think of your friend's needs and obligations, it's possible a friendship with you can't be a priority for them. A friendship cooling may not be a personal decision; you can just tell your friend, "Let's reconvene in a few months or another season." Your *about* isn't strong enough *at this time*. It may always pick up later. As long as there's desire there, anything is possible. Some scenarios where a cooling is in order:

- The friend moves away and is focused on finding a new community.
- The friend gets married and is in nesting mode.
- The friend gets divorced and is in healing mode.
- The friend enrolls in grad school and is laser focused on earning that degree.

You can say something like:

- "It sounds like you're busy, which is great. My door is always open for you. Let's touch base later in the year."
- "Congrats on all your success at work. I totally understand that your schedule is getting tighter. Drop me a line when you come back up for air."
- "Saw this article and thought of you. I know you're busy with school. I'm sending you all the good vibes. I'm proud of you for working so hard. I know it's not easy. If you ever want a study buddy, let me know. I'm happy to do work alongside you at a café if you want."
- "I'm thinking about you. No need to respond, as I know you're busy these days. If you ever want a workout buddy, let me know."

Samantha's Experience

Growing up in Long Island, musician Samantha had strong friendships. But since she's become a mom of two, she's experienced limitations on her free time. There's a certain schedule, lifestyle, and rhythm to a musician's friendships, she said. "All your friends are either there all the time and are down to hang out from noon to night because none of us have real jobs. Or they're just gone for six weeks and then you never see them again and then there's no contact other than a text or two," she told me. "Intermittent but fierce. I think that's the life of a musician's friendship."

Her circle of friends has shrunk since she's been on tour and recording a lot. "There's some needy friends who are like, 'Why don't you call me?'" she said. Others accuse her of deserting them. "They're not in that understanding mode the way other musicians are, like, 'See you in a year.'" Her nonmusician friends take her absences personally. She sees many artists get a job and move to the suburbs once they have kids.

At this point, her circle of friends are parents who make art because they understand both nap schedules and touring schedules. "It takes a very specific demographic of person to understand that level of time and emotional commitment," she said. As her circle of friends gets smaller, the understanding becomes deeper and the support becomes more meaningful.

She's also embraced project-based friendships. For instance, she started a card-playing club, and another friendship was based around publishing a zine. This way the "about" of the friendship is baked in. Now most of her friends are other musicians.

Samantha has a policy to never chase friendships no matter how much she loves the person or how close she thought they were. "I have a few friends who I just absolutely adore, think the world of, and they never call me. They never respond to my messages. And whenever I see them, they say, 'Oh my god. I'm so happy to see you.' And I'm like, 'Great! I'm also very happy to see you. But if you don't call me back, we're not hanging out.'"

Now that Samantha's in her forties, she feels much more Zen about the friendships she does have. "I feel like as you get older, or maybe if you're just more secure and confident, you no longer chase people.

So the expectations have shifted because the friend group has shrunk to people who are so similar to me: secure people who are involved in a lot of projects and are fun." One of Samantha's best friends took her as a date to a wedding. They danced, drank, and scarfed down all the food. Then, suddenly, they retreated to a small alcove and had an in-depth discussion about their philosophy of relationships. Samantha was delighted with this story, as it showed how fun and versatile her favorite friends are.

We now know the macro and micro reasons friendships crumble, so what can we do to keep the tiny flames of desire alive? The first step is to refer back to the five factors that go into why people make friends in the first place:

1. Support
2. Mating
3. Career
4. Desirable traits
5. Socializing

Just as we can decide if any of these reasons are compelling enough to maintain connection with our friends, only other people can determine if their desire in any of those areas is strong enough to necessitate connection with us. That's entirely up to them.

We can, however, work on sharpening our support skills and desirable traits and initiating enjoyable hangouts so our friends will be more likely to want to get together with us in the future.

BANISH AMBIGUITY

Say a friend blows off my text messages. My lizard brain will immediately try to search for a reason. *Maybe she's too busy with her new job to reply. Maybe she lost her phone. Maybe she hates me.* Ding ding ding! That must be it. With very little evidence, my silly brain always jumps to the worst possible conclusion. That's what people tend to do, especially if they're insecure or feel unworthy.

Having a plan to deal with scant information from others is a crucial component of being a fantastic friend. Believing (and acting upon) a self-generated story can be a relationship ruiner. We know that when faced with uncertainty, our brains like to feel reassured. We're biologically programmed to find comfort in narratives. In the absence of information (Why did my pal ghost on our plans? Why did my buddy ignore my DM?), we're often tempted to fill in the blanks ourselves (my pal doesn't care about me, my buddy thinks I'm annoying). But the problem is if you're feeling insecure or unsteady, the story you concoct is more likely to reflect those insecurities, not the truth. Perhaps your pal had a work emergency. Maybe your buddy didn't see your DM.

Mimi's Experience

Mimi told me that she finds ambiguity in a friendship to be much harder than somebody not liking you openly. That's because, she said, we're constantly trying to write the story for what someone's reaction or non-reaction means. In those dark, quiet moments, she finds herself wondering if there's something wrong with her. She can think of endless reasons why she's being rejected. It's exhausting, she said.

"Something this special shouldn't have to be so hard," she said, her voice quivering. "I shouldn't have to dance backward in heels for [a friendship] that's supposed to be with you at the very highs and the very lows."

Mimi still reels from a friend who abandoned her for an unknown reason. "I care about her so much that I've had to distance myself from really just even thinking about it because it doesn't make any sense. And I can easily say that it was a bunch of things that I did or didn't do, but then I'm not really sure if that's a productive way of thinking about it."

There's nothing like the heartbreak of losing a friend and not knowing why. In a romantic relationship, when a person dumps you, there's usually a conversation around the reasons for the breakup.

- "I'm not ready to settle down."
- "I've met someone else."
- "It's not you, it's me."
- "We want different things."

For friends, there's often no conversation around the reasons for a breakup. It just . . . deflates like a shitty soufflé. Not knowing why a friendship ended can create intense feelings of shame. *How do I explain what happened to other people? How do I explain this rupture to our mutual friends?* It's painful. And lonely too, because often, you're on an island alone with your heartbreak.

REKINDLING FRIENDSHIPS

Knowing that friendships work better if they are about something will give you a huge advantage if you're considering rekindling a lapsed friendship. Where most people go wrong is that they expect their lapsed friendships to pick up where they left off. Often, that's unrealistic. If you've had a substantial break in the friendship, you and your friend have all sorts of influences that shape your life in each other's absences, including marriage, divorce, children, caretaking, and changes in residences and jobs. Not only have you and your friend been affected by these experiences, but most likely, the core reason your friendship was based on is outdated. Maybe being from the same town and liking the same ska bands was enough to power your bond in high school, but now that you're adults, those reasons aren't compelling enough to warrant contact beyond a catch-up call or two.

Brittany's Experience

Brittany feels like she has a lot of friends. She sometimes thinks instead of going out and meeting new people, it'd be easier to return to some of her acquaintances and try to become friends with them again. Her high school friendships haven't totally fizzled, she said, but there have definitely been waves throughout the twenty years since graduation. They all have young children, which she feels is a promising hook for reconnection. "It's so nice just to chill and hang out with them," she said. "The small talk has been out of the way for twenty years, so you just hang out with them and you get right down to it. Or you don't even have to. You can just be there. There are no expectations. It's just super comfortable. I feel like with new friends, you have to do that small talk dance for a while as you're feeling each other out. But with people who have known you for a while, you don't have to do that."

Reconnecting with longtime friends can totally work for you. Just make sure you have a clear, compelling *about* present for both people and accept that things may not feel the same right off the bat. This will give your friendship the best chance to regrow.

12

Initiators, Rise Up!

Diligence is about the attention and care you put into your friendship. It's about making sure that you prioritize time together in order to keep your friendship strong, active, and healthy.

Two of my big takeaways from Dr. Langkamp's book *Practical Friendship* are: (1) we should not take our friends for granted, and (2) we should focus on making more memories with our friends.[1] The memory point caught me by surprise, honestly. Who reaches out to someone and says, "Let's make a memory"? Most people throw, say, a birthday party to feel good in the moment, not to look back on that memory of the party at some mystery date in the future.

But then Dr. Langkamp's advice clicked. All the texts in the world to a friend saying "Thinking of you!" and "Miss your face!" feel good, but they don't feel *nourishing*. There's nothing engaging our souls when reading a generic text like that.

Studies show that there is no substitute for the real deal of in-person hangout time. The spontaneity, the sense of discovery, the FUN. Imagine saying something like this to your bestie:

- "Remember when we crashed that wedding? And I danced with that guy? What was his name? Uncle Joey? Yes! Uncle Joey."

- "Remember when we rented a car and drove to Maine for a lobster roll? Then turned around and came home? We put the sunroof down and listened to Bruce Springsteen songs the whole way back."

- "Remember when we rented a cabin and danced to Robyn songs? We played 'Call Your Girlfriend' on repeat. And we made nachos on the fire? Those nachos were nasty, but we ate them anyway because we were starving."

- "Remember when we had a picnic and I brought lukewarm prosecco? We drank the whole bottle and couldn't stop petting those two labradoodles?"

- "Remember when we went to that party and I told some guy named Stephen that I was a certified alligator wrangler? I convinced him that it was a two-year online degree. I can't believe you kept a straight face the entire conversation."

Imagine yourself doubled over in laughter recalling your own version of these kinds of hijinks.

Missy's Experience
"I wish I knew how to grow new friendships better at this stage in my life. I have always found that one needs to continue to experience new things and make new memories in order to feed and grow a relationship, and sometimes that is very hard to do," she told me.

Joey's Experience
When people seek out romantic relationships, it's expected that daters will put in effort to put their best foot forward, Joey told me. "We're conditioned to see the value in putting in that work. It's the most cliché thing in the world. Everyone's like, 'Marriages are hard work,' right? And it's true. But nobody talks about friendship in those ways."

His group of guy friends has balked at the idea of putting in effort with their friendships to each other. In fact, one of his friends told the all-male group: "I don't want to put effort into our friendships because I have to put effort into my family. And I have to make an effort at work, with my wife, and my in-laws. When I hang out with you guys, I want to put in zero effort."

"And we're like, 'You have to put in a little bit.'" Joey's friend basically said no. This was a real fight they had! "I get it," Joey said to his friend. "You have to put up with a lot of people and a lot of things that are out of your control. So, when you hang out with us, you just want to do nothing. And you don't want to have to care about like, 'Oh, did that joke upset someone?' But you don't get to turn off life."

If you want true Wholehearted Friendships, you need to put effort into making happy memories together. "Friendships need to be dynamic relationships because people aren't static," Dr. Degges-White told me.[2] "And so, if I'm not willing to accept you as you change, or you're not willing to accept me as I change and grow, then that relationship's just going to be a cut-off relationship," she said. "Humans aren't static, so why do we expect relationships to be static?"

Think of a longtime friend of yours from childhood. While you might have met while you were in second grade, you still might touch base once a year or so just to see how they're doing. While your relationship began in a static period of time, it couldn't stay static. "Over time, it's become more dynamic and flexible because you're still keeping up, you're still investing energy, you're still caring about that person's well-being, and they're still caring about yours," Dr. Degges-White said.

The key is to keep the friendship balanced so both people feel cared for. "Everybody has a different capacity for friendship," Dr. Degges-White said. Some people can send handwritten cards every holiday. (Uh, not me!) Some people only manage to squeak out a text message to their best friend every two years. All people have different capacities for engagement. Some have the space, time, and money to seek connection, and others don't. Therefore, Dr. Degges-White says we should try not to get angry when you can't be a friend's number one priority.

We need to find ways to connect with friends face-to-face because it's so, so healing to be in the presence of someone who cares about us. We need a strong support network because it makes *us* feel better. "Think of when you're in the hospital and people stop by," she said. "That moment freezes the pain because you're focused on that moment." You know what I like to watch when I'm experiencing my lowest lows? Reruns of the *Jackass* TV show. I could watch Johnny Knoxville and the gang pulling ridiculous pranks on each other foreverrrrr. Friends can snap us out of our funks like that too. "And that's what friendship does," she said. "It brings a sense of pleasure. And it just hits dopamine and oxytocin and all the feel-good neurotransmitters that do good things for us."

In his book *The Art of Making Memories*, happiness researcher and chief executive of The Happiness Institute, Meik Wiking, dove deep into how powerful our happy memories can be. As part of his research, he posed a single prompt: "Please describe one of your happy memories." Over one thousand people from seventy-five countries wrote a response.

As he analyzed the responses, patterns started to emerge. There were common denominators to people's happy memories that were evident across a variety of cultures. People tended to remember experiences that were novel, meaningful, and emotional. He also found that their most powerful memories engaged the senses with vivid sights or evocative smells.

As he scrutinized the result of the Happy Memory study, Wiking identified several ingredients for making happy memories, which he calls **The Memory Manifesto**:

1. Harness the power of firsts. Seek out novel experiences and strive to make your hangouts extraordinary.

2. Make plans multisensory by going beyond visuals. Incorporate sounds, scents, touch, and tastes too.

3. Shake things up. Make your friendship hangouts as special and exciting as a romantic date.

4. Create meaningful moments by being sentimental. Bring up memories, trips, or anecdotes from your shared past that were particularly special or hilarious.

5. Share stories with one another. Start with: "Do you remember the time we . . . ?"

6. Outsource your memories. Write, photograph, record, and collect mementos from your time spent with friends that capture the peaks and struggles you endured together. [3]

"As a happiness researcher," Wiking told me over email, "I could see that our memories impact how we feel about our lives.[4] And when people are living with depression, they are not only feeling unhappy right now, but some struggle to remember anytime they were happy. To me the biggest aha moment when I wrote about happiness and memories was the understanding that we actually have a lot of power over what we—and our friends—will remember in the future."

Take the simple ingredient of attention. One of his readers told him that the chapter in his book about attention reminded her of a time she was a young girl and she was having dinner with her mother and sister. They were laughing, having a good time and feeling happy, and then suddenly her mother looked at her and her sister and said, "I hope you remember this moment."

"And here we are 30 years later, and she still remembers that moment because her mother made her pay attention to it," he told me. The act of calling attention to a moment will make it more likely for that memory to stick.

In 1932, First Lady Eleanor Roosevelt and pilot Amelia Earhart became close friends.[5] This was the same year that Earhart accomplished her iconic, record-breaking, nonstop transatlantic flight. The women met earlier that year when Roosevelt was asked to introduce Earhart at a speaking event. It's no surprise they hit it off. Both were passionate about women's rights and promoting world peace, and both had a strong interest in flying planes.

On April 20, 1933, Roosevelt invited Earhart and her husband, George Putnam, to spend the night at the White House. They had a dinner party the day of their arrival where they feasted on crab chowder and angel food cake.

During the dinner, the two women, still in their formal wear, decided to ditch the meal and take a quick spin in a twin-engine plane. The ladies went to Hoover Field and boarded an Eastern Air Transport Curtiss Condor. They weren't quite alone, as two male pilots accompanied them on the flight, as per regulations. The women took a quick flight to Baltimore and back. Roosevelt, who had applied for a student pilot license at Earhart's encouragement, copiloted part of the flight.

What I love about this story is that the desire, diligence, and delight of their friendship is on full display. They both shared a passion for flying (a clear and compelling reason that inspired them to spend time together). Roosevelt created an opportunity for them to connect (extending an invitation to dinner), and they had fun together doing something they both loved to do (delight, clearly). But more important, by getting together in person and taking a spontaneous joy ride, they made an unforgettable memory.

Maybe you need more of a sense of novelty in your friendships. Perhaps that's the missing ingredient. Wiking suggests going someplace with a friend you've never been before. Shake things up! Seek out novel experiences. Brainstorm ways to add novelty to your next hang. Think of all your senses and how to heighten them.

- Eat a cuisine that's new to you both.
- Get a manicure or pedicure.
- Go to a new coffee shop.
- Have a picnic.
- Make fancy mocktails.
- Volunteer together.
- Do a puzzle in your living room.

- Attend a lecture at a local library.

- Go to an indie bookstore. (Buy your friend a book and let them purchase a book for you.)

- Set a goal together. (e.g., Today we're going to learn how to make dirty martinis. Or poached eggs. Or chocolate babka.)

- Fantasize. (Where would we go if we could? What would we buy if we had unlimited money?)

Roosevelt and Earhart most likely didn't set out to make an impactful memory that night, but that's exactly what they did. This is why social media check-ins and text messages don't feel sustaining. Just as junk food lacks nutrition, mediating your interactions with your friends through a screen doesn't add social nourishment. In gravy terms, happy memories are the roux. They thicken the stew and add heartiness, lusciousness, and body to your friendships. We need to make more memories together, fam.

BE AN IGNITER

Dr. Franco teaches a class on loneliness. She noticed that there was one class where students got really close and hung out outside of class, while the other class didn't. She wondered what the differences were between these two classes; why was one hanging out outside of class and getting close and the other wasn't?

"I figured out that one class had an igniter, which was one person who was willing to ask everyone in the class, 'Does anyone want to go to lunch after class?' And because that one person ignited, ten other people had more friends, even though they didn't really have to do anything," she said. "In this world in which we're so passive, igniters require such a high degree of agency and activity. I feel like if we had more igniters, there would so much more infrastructure for friendships."

Igniting—inviting others to get together—is diligence in action. An igniter not only is proactive in asking people to hang out, but they also make others in the group feel like their inclusion matters. When people feel like they matter, they're more likely to participate.

Here are things a terrific igniter might say. Notice the clear and compelling reasons they offer:

- "You always have such a good read on pop culture. Want to start a monthly picnic where we share what we've been reading, watching, or listening to? Feel free to invite a few people too. Maybe we can call it a 'picnic salon.'"

- "Any interest going to a baseball game with me this summer? I don't have many girlfriends who follow local sports, and it's really fun to talk about [local sports team] with you. Do you know any other chill people who follow sports? Invite them!"

- "My local bar has a quiz night. You're so great with trivia games. Would you like to join a trivia team with me? I'd love to be on a team with you."

There's no shortage of opportunities to do stuff with cool people. Here are thirty activities friends can do together. Circle any that seem plausible for you:

1. Watch a documentary together.

2. Have a picnic.

3. Attend a concert.

4. Go for a walk around your neighborhood.

5. Go on a hike.

6. Go to a museum.

7. Take a day trip somewhere.

8. Get ice cream.

9. Do yoga together using a beginner video on YouTube.

10. Attend an author's reading.

11. Get manicures together.

12. Bumble around a Costco. Eat samples. Share a churro.

13. Attend a live podcast taping.

14. Watch a comedy special together.

15. Attend a networking event for your industry.

16. Start a painting or arts and crafts club.

17. Go on a movie date. Bring snacks.

18. Visit each other's hometown.

19. Pop into Sephora. Buy your friend a new mascara of her choice. Have her buy you a new lip gloss.

20. Grab an iced coffee and run errands together.

21. Attend a school or work event together.

22. Watch awards shows together.

23. Volunteer at a local charity.

24. Sign up for a class together.

25. Organize a clothing/perfume swap.

26. Sink some beers at a local brewery.

27. Do a puzzle together.

28. Join a local sports league.

29. Bake cookies together and take them to a mutual friend.

30. Go on a double date.

SAY YES TO THINGS PEOPLE ASK YOU TO DO!

As a researcher, people always ask Dr. Hall what the secret is for friendships. It's actually dead simple: don't be a flake. "Respond. Show up. Say yes," he said.

He asked me a question: "If I invite you, Anna, to hang out with me, how many times am I going to do that before I stop if you never say yes? Once? If I say 'Hey, look, we should go do this,' and you're like, 'No, I'm busy. I'd love to, but I'm busy,' or you put me off or you never respond, I'd be like, 'Oh, she doesn't really want to hang out with me.'"

Think about if a friend from work asks you to get together outside of work one day, or to come over and meet their family, and you blow them off. "I don't think it takes many no's before a person stops asking," he said. "So if you think about that negative spiral, how quickly it goes from invitation to nothing, it's a cliff."

We have to stop being so flaky with one another, Dr. Hall said: "And I'm not trying to throw people under the bus. People are busy. But if people say, 'Do you want to go out and do something?' Say yes and show up."

And if it's not your favorite thing in the world to do, Dr. Hall said, suggest something you'd like to do next time. If you have to reschedule, make sure to reschedule in that moment. Reschedule right now. Be intentional about your choices.

We live in a culture where putting people off about plans is the norm, but that's not an excuse to perpetuate it. "So there's a fun little anecdote from intercultural communication classes that one of the things that they educate people from other countries about when they talk to Americans is that when Americans say, 'We should get together,' they do not mean that," Dr. Hall said. "And cultures are confused or like, 'Well, that's personal. Like, that's a pretty big intimate request to get together.' And what they have to learn is it doesn't mean anything in our culture. And what's a shame about that, to me, is I think we detect the possibility of relationship development all of the time. I think we do something about it nearly never."

A big hurdle, he said, is that when people start a new job, go to a new school, or move to a new place, they're starting from scratch. "They're not accustomed to having to start again and build the process of friendship, commit the hours, follow through, and keep doing it. Then they find themselves in a situation where they also haven't been keeping in touch with the people from wherever they were before. And now they're in a bad spot."

For those who begin friendships feeling anxious about rejection, Dr. Hall has empathy for you. If you have expectations that friendships should fall into place naturally, you will be at a disadvantage. "Because no one's ready-made. There is no such thing as a ready-made friend that just shows up and does what you want, which is actually in some ways why friendship is great," Dr. Hall said. "They're their own person that chooses to be with you and is different enough from you to help you grow and change and become who you're going to be. So you actually wouldn't want somebody who is just the mirror image of you and does everything you want because that would be miserable. That's like a *Black Mirror* episode."

THE EVOLUTION OF A COLD CALL

Jasmine's Experience

Jasmine loves sending a cold outreach email to people in both her personal and professional lives. "We apply all these really great strategies to our work lives, but we act like they don't actually belong in our personal lives," she told me. Jasmine actually messaged me out of the blue a few years ago. "I admired your work," she said, "and I wanted you to know that I did. I had no expectation, no intention. I just wanted you to know that your work made a difference to me."

"Now, most people will read something and think it touched them but not take that extra step. So, when you do that, if you're genuine and someone's genuine back, you can create a relationship with that," she said. "But you have to invest in it. You can't just have one [social media] exchange and call it a day."

None of us are born communication experts. In fact, here are some DMs I've sent to people I've admired. They've been edited slightly to remove any identifying information. But this is an accurate representation of me sashaying into inboxes with varying degrees of success.

Here is the message I sent a local Philly blogger in 2010:

Me: Hey, Harry! I read your stuff all the time, and I'm not sure if we've ever met, but I wanted to introduce myself. Hi! My name is Anna.
Harry: Anna great to DM-meet you haha. Thx for reading! I read your blog & find it hilarious!

If I had to rate this message, I'd give it a 1/10. It gets a one because I at least spelled *Harry*'s name correctly. That should count for something. Otherwise, it's totally bland. No information is offered. I didn't give him a call to action, as marketers call it. I don't let him know why I'm reaching out: Do I want to help him in his career? Do I want to meet for coffee or lunch? No one knows! I certainly didn't help him understand why we were talking.

Here's how I reached out to people in 2017. It's not much better, I have to say. *collar tug*

Me: Hi Marcy! Not to sound cheesy, but you inspire me as an author and freelance writer. As I figure out my 2018 goals, I looked at what you've accomplished and it's spurred me on. Keep up the incredible work. Cheers!

Marcy: wow thank you so much! this is especially good timing because i'm having one of those days where i feel like i can't get anything done, so thank you! <3 You keep up the awesome work, too :)

To no one's surprise, nothing really happened after I sent this message. We didn't become friends. We didn't grow closer as colleagues. Nada. A few months later, I tried reaching out to her again. I clearly learned nothing and basically repeated my strategy of just saying hello with no clear or compelling reason offered.

Me: Hi Marcy! I just wanted to say congrats on having a wildly successful year. I always perk up when I see something you've written. I'm inspired by your terrific work. Have a wonderful holiday!! xoxo

Marcy: aw, thank you so so much! congrats on all your great stuff this year, too! <3 happy holidayssss xoxo

I give my messages to her a 2/10. It was like a drive-by hello, not an attempt at fostering an ongoing relationship. I wasn't getting any traction, and I wasn't sure why.

Once I'd been a full-time freelance journalist for a few years, I upped my game with cold calls. Here's what I said when I reached out to a reporter I admired on the West Coast:

Me: Hey Kathleen! Hello from Philly. I'm a huge fan of your work. I signed up for your newsletter and encouraged a few other of my writer friends to sign up too. I'm really enjoying it. Keep up the great work!

This message is a 5/10. Kathleen replied cheerfully, and we eventually started a virtual group with a few other freelance writers. This message was successful in that I offered her something: spreading the word about her newsletter. I did something for her, which made her feel inclined to ask how she could help me in return. We're still friendly to this day.

I reached out to a fellow freelancer named Molly in 2019. Look how easy I made it for her to say yes to me. I was learning!

Me: Hey Molly!! Wanna have a phone date? I'd love to learn more about you and what you're working on. When's good? I'm free anytime tmrw and Wed. between 10am - 4pm EST. Hopefully we can connect soon!

I rate this message a solid 8/10. This is leaps and bounds better than anything I've ever done when reaching out to a semi-stranger. Here's another message I sent, this time to a local writer who wrote a cover story for *Philadelphia* magazine about being child-free.

Me: Hi Jessie!!! I've been following you for a while. I see we both live in Philly. Where do you live?
Jessie: Hi Anna!! I have been following you too, so it's so great to hear from you! I'm in [redacted]. We should hang out and talk writing IRL sometime.
Me: I'd love to meet for coffee or lunch. I'm free anytime on Friday 2/28 or Sunday 3/1.

In this case, my reason for reaching out was clear and compelling: we're both writers in the same area, and we cover a similar beat. As a result, we still have a nice, supportive friendship today, and we get together at least once a season.

This is how I reached out to a woman who announced she was working on a nonfiction book at the same time I wrote this one:

Me: Congrats, Heather!!! I just announced my book deal today. It seems like we're on similar timelines too as mine is slated to come out in Spring 2024. That's so cool!!!! I'm here for you if you need anything. I'm happy to share media leads and be a moral support to you . . . anything that would be helpful.

Heather: SAME! It's been such a journey to get to this place and I have NO IDEA what to expect, especially when it comes to writing a reported book - all my friends got away with selling straight memoirs.

The result? Heather and I became book buddies as I penned this very tome you have in your hands. We had weekly check-in meetings to share our struggles with the writing process. Our book buddy-ness started because I reached out with an offer to help her. "This is the way," says *The Mandalorian*, and also me.

In the more successful examples, I highlighted what I liked about the other person and why we should be in touch. Doing this makes people feel like they matter, which will make it more likely that they'll say yes to my invitation to connect. Or, if it's not a yes, hopefully they'll make a counteroffer with an activity or level of connection they would feel comfortable with.

Exercise: Cold Call Boot Camp

Think of one to three friends you'd like to hang out with, and let's practice crafting messages to spark connection. In each one, be sure to explain who you are, why you're reaching out, and what you hope to see happen.

Here's a real-life example to help get you started.

A woman with a popular podcast just moved into my neighborhood. Obviously, I think she's cool as hell and would love to be friends. Let's see if I can wrangle a friend date.

I. Friend's name: Marsha

Who I am: Hi Marsha! My name is Anna Goldfarb. I'm a friendship journalist. Yes, that's a thing.

Why I'm reaching out: We're neighbors. *waves hello from down the street*

What I hope to see happen: I usually pop into [our local café] to write. Any interest in joining me for an iced coffee? I'd love to hear about your work and why you moved to Philly.

As far as a cold call, it's pretty solid. It's casual enough that hopefully she'll take me up on the offer. Now you try! Complete this exercise for as many potential friends as you can think of.

II. Friend's name:

_____

Who you are:

_____

Why you're reaching out:

_____

What you hope to see happen:

_____

Dropping a line to someone you don't know doesn't have to be a fraught thing. Your goal is to get to a yes as quickly as possible. To do that, you have to make your case for why getting together (or meeting) will be compelling for the other person.

Dr. Franco has benefited from being an igniter. In fact, she started a group for a small group of a few writers and added me to it! Yes, it can be hard to be the igniter. You might have to do more logistical work of organizing, like sending emails and taking polls on when's best to meet. But, you also have more sway over the objective. You get to decide what the group is focused on and curate the people involved.

These hangouts you've ignited, Dr. Franco said, will also help you get more social interaction in your life. This is good news, especially if you've been letting your social life languish the past few years. Ideally, this group would meet regularly. "That way nobody has to be like, 'Hey, is anyone free to hang out?'" she said. "It's baked in that you meet, say, every other Tuesday. And so the social interaction is embedded rather than having to be sought after."

Kelly's Experience

When it comes to maintaining friendships, "It's impossible unless you're willing to take a chance at connection," Kelly, a writer, told me. "I met one of my best friends (also a writer) on Twitter. I realized we lived in the same city and I DMed her and asked if she wanted to meet up for coffee. We never would've crossed paths if I hadn't put myself out there."

Kelly did everything right. She reached out to a peer, gave a reason to meet ("We're both writers"), and they made it happen.

WHEN YOU'RE NOT HAPPY WITH ALWAYS BEING THE IGNITER

You may get to a point where you feel let down that you're the one always rallying a crew. You're the one creating the experience, which, let's be real, is unpaid labor. It can get old when it feels like you're pulling in people who matter to you, but no one is reciprocating the feeling.

Lauren's Experience

"I wish my friends would initiate more hangouts," Lauren told me. "I'm almost always the one initiating. I don't think it's that they don't like me because they usually accept the invite and we have a nice time! But it feels like the onus is usually on me to make things happen."

If there's one part about friendship that elicits the most groans it's accepting that fact that we all have to initiate hangouts with our friends. I can practically hear you yelling at me, "Anna, I'm SO busy. You don't even know. Now you're trying to add more things to my plate? IN THIS ECONOMY???"

You don't have to do anything. If you're happy with how your friendships are, you do you. But if you're missing connection in your life, if you miss having friendly faces you see regularly, then something has to change. Why not try this igniting thing?

It might take a few tries to find the right group. You may not hit it out of the park on your first go-round. Maybe the pinball league you started is a flop. Or the Jurassic Park Appreciation Society you created disbanded after one meetup. That may happen. Maybe there's not enough Ian Malcolm fans in your town. Their loss, honestly. Try something else. Keep at it until you find a passionate group of friends geeking out about the same thing and something gels.

Abby's Experience

A woman named Abby told me, "I wish I knew how to organize my life better so that making room for people in my life didn't feel like an imposition." She feels chronically stressed and overwhelmed and like she barely has time to herself. Then, she said, she prioritizes weekends and evenings with her partner, and it doesn't feel easy to add people in to the mix.

"I know there's got to be something I can do to take better control of my life to make it feel more possible and not like a chore," she said. "I know it will take intention and effort and it won't be effortless, but I don't want it to feel like pulling teeth." She wishes she knew how to make herself more available, how to feel more expansive so she can be present with others she's trying to bring into her life.

I know, Abby. I do not give this advice lightly. The tweak I'd suggest is to focus on only one or two people who seem promising and find ways to connect with them. You don't have to create an entire social network out of thin air.

I'd also remind you (again) that this friend thing is 100 percent optional! If your desire is weakened or isn't there, then diligence and delight aren't going to happen in that relationship.

It's such a cruel paradox: we need to rely on our friends precisely when we feel stretched thin because they will help our load feel lighter. "Conversing with a friend just once during the day to catch up, joke around, or tell them you're thinking of them can increase your happiness and lower your stress level by day's end," Dr. Hall said in a study he co-wrote.[6]

As much as you may strive to be the diligent friend who remembers to send a gift every birthday or mark every momentous occasion in your friends' lives, you may not be that person. When juggling work commitments and household obligations, how can you possibly manage to make sure your friends also feel loved and secure? It's understandable to feel busy, but busyness is a choice. When you're snowed under, it's even more important to be a considerate friend. You don't want your friends to be left to make sense of your silence. If your friends don't know where they stand with you, they're liable to make up their own (likely inaccurate) stories about why you're not available.

Michelle's Experience

"I wish I knew how to prioritize friends," Michelle told me. "I'm friendly, and I often find myself gaining a friend I didn't necessarily want. So now I've got a new friend trying to hang out, and I haven't even seen my long-term friends in months. But if I want this new friendship to grow, I've got to hang, but then what about my college buddy? Who do I prioritize?"

Tal's Experience

Tal wants queer friends, but her shyness is an obstacle. "When going to queer events, I feel like no one will like me or I'm too shy to go up to someone," she said. "Social events intimidate me, so going to them to specifically meet new people is a real challenge for me. I feel lost about how else to go about it."

"If I could make people do one thing," friendship coach Danielle Bayard Jackson told me, "it would be to take initiative with scheduling hangouts. I don't think it's a matter of laziness, but fear."[7] The podcast host and author of *Fighting for Our Friendships* sees how debilitating this anxiety can be.

"You're missing a friend? Call her," she said. "You have a sense that she's overwhelmed? Go to her house. You know you want to rekindle the friendship, but you're scared that she's mad at you? Reach out. You think that girl at your job is really cool, but you don't think she really likes you? Go out for lunch."

"So many friendships die on the table," Bayard Jackson said. "They end before they even begin because we are scared of rejection." If she could wave a wand and fix things, she'd want people to swallow their fear, take the plunge, and reach out anyway.

People are starved for connection. Just as Dorothy could click her heels three times to return home, reaching out to friends with a compelling reason to meet is the way to find the connection we're craving.

Gianna's Experience

Gianna discovered that if she doesn't invest in her friendships, then they will not continue to grow. She mentors people at work, helping them to fulfill their potential by giving them feedback and praising them. "I think that we have to do the same things for our friendships if we want them to thrive too," she said. "When someone reaches out to me unexpectedly, and says something that is really touching to me, I'm just so glad that they thought of me. I will tell them, 'It really means a lot that you reached out to me. That you called me on your walk home from taking the kids from school. That even if you didn't know if you could reach me or if

I would answer, that you tried it anyway.' Because I think that's important to encourage people to do it again."

IF YOU'RE SCARED OF REJECTION, TURN THE TABLES

Ellen Hendriksen, clinical psychologist and the author of *How to Be Yourself: Quiet Your Inner Critic and Rise Above Social Anxiety*, says one way to prepare yourself for rejection is to "turn the tables," as she calls it.[8] If a friend reached out to you and said, "Hey, let's go for a walk or hop on a call," how would you feel? Most likely, Dr. Hendriksen said, you'd feel delighted, or even flattered, that a friend reached out and suggested a get-together. Likewise, an invitation you propose could spread the same excitement to others. Hopefully this reframe will help you realize that your anxiety is out of proportion to the event.

When she asks her clients to imagine themselves as the recipient to an invitation, inevitably they say, "Oh, that would be awesome. I would love it if they reached out to me." Their anxiety about having their invitations rejected comes from the uncertainty of the outcome. "It comes from not knowing what's going to happen, not knowing what the right thing to do is," Dr. Hendriksen said. "And so if you introduce the scenario where they answer, they know they'll feel delighted and then that anxiety usually goes away."

THINK OF REJECTION AS A LAYOVER NOT A DESTINATION

When a friend tells you something like "Now's not a good time," it could mean they are busy. Or they're ill. Or they have a variety of other things going on. "But it doesn't mean that that's a rejection of you and your friendship," Dr. Henricksen said. "It's a situation that might feel like rejection and is not a personal rejection, necessarily."

If you're new to initiating, start small. Send a voice memo text. Share a happy memory between you two. An interesting article. A sentimental song. A silly meme.

What if I reach out and I don't hear back?

This means your friend is most likely not in your Jacuzzi and is more likely in your swimming pool or bonfire party. For a friend to be a vital friend, they need to get back to you in a reasonable time frame. I don't make the rules here. Part of being a vital friend is reciprocal communication. My slogan: no reciprocal communication, no vital friendship! It's a mouthful. I'm still workshopping it.

WHAT IF I DON'T HAVE ENOUGH GREAT FRIENDS?

This is only a problem if you're unhappy about it. Many people feel like one or two friends is enough for them. That's totally fine. You might have friendships at work, with your pets, with children or relatives who play vital roles for you.

If you're unhappy with the number of friends you have, consider reconnecting with people in your bonfire or water park. As long as you offer a clear and compelling reason to connect, you can see if it's a promising fit. Sometimes just saying out loud: "I want more friends to do x with" is enough to snap you into action.

Exercise: How to Not Take Rejection Personally

People tend to internalize rejection as a reflection of their self-worth. It's an easy trap to fall into. However, in most cases, rejection is often not a personal rebuke. It may be influenced by external factors we don't have much information about. This is actually one lesson you learn when freelancing. Editors may say no to a pitch I send, and I know it's not a reflection of the worthiness of my idea. It might get rejected because they're already working on a similar story. Or their budget was slashed and they can't afford to assign me the piece. Or they're working on an upcoming package so my story doesn't have a place on the editorial calendar. It happens all the time. What do I do when my idea is rejected? I pitch it somewhere else. That's the nature of the game. Social invitations are no different.

For this exercise, we're going to challenge our tendency to take rejection personally by considering alternative reasons for the rebuff.

For instance:

I. Friend #1: "Want to go to the movies with me?"

Friend #2: "I can't."

Come up with three reasons Friend #2 can't attend that aren't personal:

1. She can't find childcare.
2. She can't afford to go to the movies right now.
3. She started a new medicine and has been having migraines. She's worried she'll get sick while we're out.

Now you try!

II. Friend #1: "Want to come over for a drink?"

Friend #2: "I can't."

Come up with three reasons Friend #2 can't attend that aren't personal:

1. _____

2. _____

3. _____

Now, recall times you asked a friend to do something and your friend declined.

III. The invitation:

_____

_____

Friend's response:

_____

_____

Come up with three reasons your friend couldn't attend that aren't personal:

1. _____

2. _____

3. _____

IV. The invitation:

_____

_____

Friend's response:

_____

_____

Come up with three reasons your friend couldn't attend that aren't personal:

1. _____

2. _____

3. _____

My hope is that by depersonalizing the rejection, you'll take some of the sting out of being told no. Humans are messy creatures who aren't always the best at being forthcoming about why they can't do something. Please give your friends—especially your bathtub, Jacuzzi, and swimming pool friends—the benefit of the doubt. Assume a rejection isn't personal unless they explicitly tell you otherwise. That's part of the trust you extend as their close friend.

Hopefully by completing these exercises, you will resist the urge to take others' decisions personally and liberate yourself from that mental and emotional anguish. In the next chapter, we'll continue building our resilience in friendships by cultivating a flexible mindset and appreciating the way our friendships look today. Yes, even the flawed ones.

13

The Unbeatable Power
of a Flexible Mindset

I love a good emotional car wreck. As a kid, sometimes I'd fake being sick so I could stay home and watch a truly wild lineup of late '80s, early '90s talk shows: Donahue, Oprah, Sally Jessy Raphael, Jenny Jones, Ricki Lake, and Jerry Springer. Brazen New York City club kids, pissed off goths, belligerent cheaters, jilted lovers; I'd watch it all. Give me a box of Little Debbie Swiss Rolls and free run of the television during the daytime hours and I felt so completely entertained, I could enjoy that high for weeks.

My rubbernecking extended to advice columns too. I'd religiously read the daily "Dear Abby" columns in the paper after I scanned the comics section. Here, petty injustices took center stage, with Abby being the supreme arbiter of what was okay and what wasn't. Jealous sisters-in-law, clueless spouses, self-righteous neighbors: I'd read every word. These squabbles were a much more sustainable hit, a microdose of dysfunction for me to ogle.

Now, one of my favorite online advice columns is *Slate's* "Dear Prudence," and one recent letter stood out to me.[1] Buckle up, because this one's a doozy.

In this letter, a man had recently run across racy photos of his wife with her high school and college boyfriends while transferring files from an old computer to a new one. This made him jealous. Not because she had sexual relationships with them or loved them, he explained. "I got jealous because it shows an amount of effort that I feel is missing, particularly in our intimate life," he wrote. "She put on makeup, put on an outfit, took pictures, sexually experimented with them," he complained. She did these things to impress these guys.

As her husband, he felt entitled to that same amount of effort. He "asked, nagged, pleaded, begged, bribed, and guilted her into doing a fraction of that," which only tanked his self-worth and sent him into depression. His question to Prudence aka Jenée Desmond-Harris: "I know she puts forth so much effort on all the other fronts of her life in order to make a great life for her kids and family that it physically and emotionally exhausts her. Can I ask for more without being selfish?"

Ms. Desmond-Harris replied with a brilliant, and possibly controversial, answer. She suggested the man re-create his wife's situation in high school and college when she had all the time in the world to apply makeup and take racy pictures. He should make more money so she can quit her job and focus on herself. Taking kids and the household chores off her plate will help things too. Next, he should create those kinds of relationships she had when she was younger, when she felt cool and her body was more fit. And, the trickiest part, he should become someone she desires and wants to impress.

"The guys from her past liked her exactly as she was," she wrote, "so you'll have to convey that you think she's perfect now. In short: become a completely different person in a way that's impossible given your current reality, and who knows, maybe she will, too."

In this case, the letter writer thought his problem was his wife's effort. But really, his problem was his own unrealistic expectations he held toward her.

Is anyone else having a LIGHT BULB MOMENT right now? How many times have we beaten ourselves up thinking we're horrible friends, that we don't reach out to others enough. That we're not proactive enough about putting a get-together on the calendar.

The reality is that *we* aren't the same people we were when we began these friendships so many years ago. Maybe our capacity to devote ourselves to friendships has changed because our commitments and obligations have shifted. Maybe the foundation for the friendship itself has mutated or evolved. We must adjust our expectations for ourselves and others when it comes to our friendships today.

One of the most helpful things I can tell you about navigating your adult friendships is that embracing flexible expectations towards your friends is a gift you give yourself. Don't get me wrong, giving grace to others makes other people enjoy being friends with you too. But for *you* to enjoy the people in your life, you need to make sure your expectations are in line with reality.

Expectations are the experiences, feelings, and thoughts we predict will happen in our lives. We have expectations for ourselves—the achievements we hope to accomplish, and the milestones we hope we experience. We have expectations when it comes to our education, our careers, our love life, our family relationships. We have expectations for our routines, our pets, and our close friends too. For example, I expect my husband to scratch my back when I ask him to, and I expect my cat, Eleanor, to curl up on my lap while I watch television.

Fixed expectations are rigid, narrow, and myopic. Success is black and white: you either achieve the objective or you don't. These expectations tend to fixate on goals with variables outside of one's control. A fixed expectation could look like:

- If I don't get this promotion, I'm a failure.
- If I don't finish this race, I'm a loser.
- If I don't have ten people wish me a happy birthday, then I'm a pathetic dud with no friends.

In these cases of black-and-white thinking, there's no room for nuance, self-compassion, or gratitude. What if you don't get a promotion because the company had a bad quarter and they aren't offering any employees advancement? What if you don't finish the race due to a medical emergency or weather event? What if you had three people who love you ferociously wish you a happy birthday?

On the other hand, flexible expectations are open, curious, and dynamic. They are responsive to new information and adjust accordingly. They are aware of what forces are in their control and what forces aren't. They work harder to find updated definitions of what success looks like and are proactive about protecting one's headspace.

Reality is what is *actually* happening in your life. It's the cold splash of water on our faces when life doesn't go as planned. For instance, although my husband did scratch my back when I asked him to **insert praise hands emoji**, Eleanor wasn't feeling cuddly and instead chose to sleep on her throne of soft blankets instead of my lap.

To varying levels, my expectations both were and were not met. That's life! We deal with that all the time. Whenever I encounter a curveball (an unexpected phone call, lack of kitty cuddles), I adjust accordingly.

Of course, when we have more rigid expectations for ourselves and others, it can be harder to cope when our expectations and reality don't align. There is a saying, "Expectation is the root of all heartache." And honestly? That's been pretty true for me. When my expectations aren't met, disappointment, sadness, anger, and pain typically occur.

For instance, here are some expectations I've had lately:

I. **Expectation for a chronically late friend:** My friend said she's on her way to pick me up. But I know she runs late, so I won't put my shoes on until she texts me she's outside.

Reality: She was a few minutes late and texted me she was outside. I didn't bat an eyelash.

Emotional result: I felt totally fine and was happy to see her.

My expectations were: Flexible and realistic.

II. **Expectation for my goals as an author:** My first book, a humor memoir about being terrible at dating, will be a bestseller that will bring me fame and fortune.

Reality: I didn't achieve fame or fortune, LOL. Sales were okay, but I didn't earn my advance out.

Emotional result: I felt like a failure, and I was ashamed.

My expectations were: Way too rigid. I didn't consider other definitions of success and what that could look like.

III. Expectation for my educational career: Earning a grad school degree will give me a leg up in the marketplace.

Reality: I still struggled to find work after grad school, as my degree priced me out of more junior positions that I would've been happy to take.

Emotional result: Bitterness and shame. I felt like I wasted my time and money on an advanced degree that didn't move the needle for my career in the way I'd hoped it would in the time frame I wanted.

My expectations were: Rigid as fuck. Just because you earn a degree doesn't mean you'll automatically find work in your field. Also, I graduated in 2008, smack-dab in the middle of a global economic crisis, which severely impacted my opportunities.

IV. Expectation for my personal life: Being married will make all my problems disappear.

Reality: Marriage is not a magic eraser. Problems still exist even though I'm married. I've learned to approach problems as a team with my husband so surmounting life's trials feels more manageable.

Emotional result: Humbled. I have a new, more mature understanding of what marriage is.

My expectations were: Naïve. A touch unrealistic too.

The more rigid my expectations, the more likely I'll feel stronger, more complicated emotions when they aren't met. All high expectations come with this risk. Having flexible, realistic expectations of myself and others puts *me* in a better mood and protects me from pain, disillusionment, and disappointment. The key is to strike a balance between setting sky-high ambitious goals and accepting that setbacks are a natural part of life. We all have to figure out what that balance looks like in our own lives.

When we hold fixed expectations in our friendships and refuse to incorporate new information we're receiving, we set ourselves up for heartache. For instance, you might expect your best friend to be all things to you. "We may want a friend to be our mother, our therapist and our psychic all rolled up into one," the authors of the book *Toxic Friendships* wrote.[2] "While it may be normal to occasionally want that support, it is not normal to receive it from a single person."

"Friends cannot provide an unending supply of praise, patience, encouragement, comfort, or reassurance," the authors added. "Just like you, they can hit the 'emotional empty' mark."

When it comes to friendships, people may not fully grasp "that they're dealing with another person who's very complex. And [the friendship] might not fit the scenario of the movies they've seen or *Sex and the City*. You know, the cliché of those four friends like that," said Jan Yager, a sociologist and friendship expert. "Those images are very powerful. They're also inaccurate."

In reality, friendships endure all sorts of variations in intimacy.

Meredith's Experience

"I am an introvert, and I'm severely chronically ill, so I love having friends I can ignore for a while when I'm overwhelmed," Meredith told me. "I know I can call them out of the blue and reconnect. They know they can do the same. But we can each live our lives independently for a while when needed." For her, she doesn't expect constant communication, so she's not disappointed when she doesn't get it.

Fran's Experience

"There's lots of pressure to hang out all the time," Fran told me. "I am one of those people who are completely fine going for weeks or months without a hang. But a lot of my friends have become *so needy*, wanting to hang out every week or constantly making plans." This neediness makes her feel bogged down. "I'd rather have more spontaneous hangs," she said. "I am someone who recharges when I'm alone."

In her friendship coaching business, Ms. Bayard Jackson has noticed that a lot of her clients—mostly high-achieving women—aren't satisfied with their friendships. The reason given is that they are concerned about having to share an expectation they have for their friend. They feel that, seeing as how they're friends, the buddy should just automatically know their desires. They shouldn't need to have expectations spelled out. Instead, close friends should miraculously intuit what the expectations for the friendship are. These troubled clients resent having to share their expectations at all. In fact, in their minds, the need to share their expectation is evidence of a less intense bond.

"If I expect that because you're a woman, you should get it, and then you don't get it, then I am going to draw conclusions about the capacity of our friendship," Bayard Jackson said.

Think of a person who resists being explicit with what gift they want for their birthday. They want gift givers to purchase the right item without their saying what it is because that, to them, is evidence of strong interpersonal intimacy. "But the risk that I run when I choose not to tell you what I want for my birthday, is you that you won't give me what I want," Bayard Jackson said. "And so here we are on this line of like, 'I shouldn't have to say it, but then if I don't say it, I might not get what I want. But if she's my friend then she'll know.'"

These assumptions and unspoken expectations set us up for failure. We are not clairvoyant. Until a tech billionaire devises a way for us to download each other's thoughts, we have to rely on good old-fashioned communication. If you expect other people to guess your thoughts, needs, and preferences, you will be sorely disappointed.

A lot of people feel like articulating what they would like to see happen somehow detracts from the chemistry they have with friends, Bayard Jackson said. That thinking is, frankly, bullshit. If you expect your friends to know that you want to be magically whisked away for a wine tasting for your birthday, you're going to be eternally disappointed with the world. To get what you want in a situation, you absolutely have to share your expectations: "For my birthday this year, I would really love to have a wine tasting with you at that new winery I saw on Instagram. You in?"

I don't know much about football, but I do know that the team has a huddle where they outline the play they'll execute. This is what sports movies have taught me. If the players didn't do this, if nobody on the team was on the same page, it would be mayhem! Our friendships need huddles too:

- Instead of hoping your friend guesses what you'd like to do to celebrate a work milestone, say, "Here's the plan: To celebrate this achievement, I would really love to get dinner with you. You game?"

- Instead of replying that you can't make your friend's party, give some additional context: "I can't make it to your housewarming party because I have a family barbecue that day. Can I come over another time to see your new place?"

- Instead of stewing that you haven't seen your friend and she hasn't reached out to you, say: "I want to get together with you more regularly. How can we spend more time together? Any ideas?"

Remember at the beginning of the book I told you that friendships require maturity? Sharing your expectations with others is a mature thing to do. It shows you understand the realities of adult friendships, and you are a wonderful teammate to your close friend.

By the way, being flexible doesn't mean pretending you don't have needs and that you're super chill. Rather, Bayard Jackson said it's about being open and flexible to (1) what friendship looks like now, and (2) who might become your friends.

"A lot of us have preconceived ideas about what a friend should look like and how old she should be," she said. She encourages us to be open-minded about who might come into our social orbit. "Allow yourself to be surprised and delighted by connections," she said.

You might resent having to update your expectations about both other people and your own friendships at this stage in life. Perhaps you liked having your expectations the way they were. Maybe it's painful to admit that life has changed us in unpredictable ways. It's scary, right?

- I always hear from my best friend on my birthday. I don't want to let that expectation go.

- I loved having Tuesday night happy hour with my friend. I'm sad we don't do that as often anymore.

- I enjoyed having hour-long phone calls with my best friend, but that's changed since she's been married (or had a kid, or scored that promotion).

But holding resentment about having to update your expectations is not going to bring you closer to other people. It will only frustrate you and alienate you from others.

Here are how some of my expectations have changed for my friends. In my twenties, I expected my friends to:

- Help me move across town for free.

- Listen to me complain about my exes *ad infinitum*.

- Be punctual to our hangouts.

- Attend my birthday party (this was nonnegotiable).

- Overlook my foibles like gossiping and being a cheapskate. (Sorry, friends! I'm better now, I swear.)

In my thirties, I expected my friends to:

- Return my calls, emails, and texts within twenty-four hours. If I didn't hear back, I'd assume we were in a fight.

- Attend my group birthday dinner at a fancy-ish restaurant. (Now, I'd rather die than expect my friends to split a check eleven ways.)

- Take an interest in my work. I'd be hurt if they didn't notice or acknowledge my professional success.

In my forties, I now expect my friends to:

- Return a text message within seventy-two hours, give or take. I don't automatically assume malice if I don't hear back at all. I just assume that my message got lost in the shuffle or that they're busy.

- Give me grace when I don't check in for long stretches of time.

- Not take long silences on my end personally. I also would hope that they'd give me the benefit of the doubt and assume my intentions are always good.

- Gift me presents if they're moved to. Gifts are never expected but always appreciated.

- Affirm our love and affection for each other when we do connect.

What's interesting to me when I look over this list is that the standards I set for myself changed. I transitioned from having expectations of what friends did for me (helping *me* move, take an interest in *my* work, lavish *me* with attention on *my* birthday) to what *I* need from my friends (lots of leeway, sporadic bouts of affirmation). It's a shift. I attribute this change to maturity; I've come to realize that I'm not the center of the universe. Other people have full lives with more pressing obligations and commitments.

In a perfect world, what would you need to become the ultimate super-friend who has endless energy to catch up with your array of besties? More hours in the day? An assistant? A babysitter available 24/7? Piles of money? Your friends probably wish they had more resources too. The reality for all of us is that there are only so many hours in a day, and we only have so much time to dedicate to others' needs. Like the letter writer who wrote into "Dear Prudence," you might be holding your loved one to an impossible standard they aren't realistically able to meet.

Updating your expectations will give both people in the friendship more freedom because it shows you're open to growing together.

I needed to change my expectations of others and embrace realistic friendships, not fantasy friendships. My friends won't always be available to answer my phone calls or reply to my messages. It doesn't mean they don't love me; it just means that I can't be their priority in the moment. Not forever. Just for *right now*.

Part of being a wholehearted friend is to assume you—and all your friends—would prioritize each other more if you had endless resources. But we don't have those endless resources. So, let's give each other the benefit of the doubt, yes?

Holding outdated expectations causes us pain because our brains are prediction machines. We're programmed to want to know what's coming down the pike. But life isn't predictable; it throws us curveballs all the time. Inexplicable things happen in the world. People, by their nature, are unpredictable. We're biologically programmed to search for meaning even when the information we have is inaccurate or incomplete.

TV shows and movies give us a distorted or incomplete picture of what adult friendships look like, which only confuses us further. Shows like *Friends*, and *Golden Girls* show friendship monogamy, where a group of friends stick together no matter what. That might work when you need character arcs, but that's not real life. In real life, people get sick. They get depressed. Distracted. Busy. They have other shit going on.

Misaligned expectations will put a strain on your relationships and create conflict. They will also interfere with your ability to feel gratitude. You will not be able to appreciate what you have in front of you because you're so focused on what's missing. If you're hoping to have several hours of uninterrupted time with your best friend, you're going to feel like crap about the half hour a friend has to catch up with you. You might be so focused on what your friendship *is not* that you can't appreciate what your friendship *is*.

We can't superglue our friendships in place, preserving them in time like a pinned butterfly in a museum exhibit. But how we *feel* about these changes ARE under our control.

It's one thing to carry expectations for yourself, but when you carry expectations for other people, you need to share them. That can feel scary. You know who didn't communicate their expectations? Molly Ringwald's Samantha in *Sixteen Candles*! She moped around the entire movie bemoaning how no one in her teenage orbit remembered her birthday. But did she pipe up about how excited she was? Did she give others a chance to get excited with her? Sorry, Samantha, but some of the buffoonery of your sixteenth birthday is on you.

If you had wonderful, dynamic friendships in young adulthood, it can feel hollow or strange to have different-looking friendships today. You might feel like something is missing, like your friendships aren't what they *should* be. They're not as intimate, not as spontaneous, not as fun.

Lakshmi's Experience

Lakshmi went on a five-day girls' trip with her two best friends to Charleston, South Carolina, for her fiftieth birthday. None of the women had visited Charleston before. The location was perfect because there was "just enough to do but not so much to do that you can't just sit around a lot," she told me. "We would just sit and talk for hours on end." What struck her most was how fun it was "to be back in that little kid mode" of talking endlessly over a few days as opposed to a quick catch-up on the phone. "I know it's hard to coordinate that time for all of us to get away, but I really cherished those couple of days." She wishes we all could all do more of what she calls the "rambling times," where friends can truly decompress and share.

We did that much more in our twenties, right? "When's the last time you wanted to have a brunch?" she asked me. "I haven't gone out for brunch in probably 15 years. Where you just sit there for hours over eggs and have a drink or two or three, or too much coffee, or whatever, and just hang out for hours and just talk about whatever."

She told me, "I don't have time for brunch anymore. Like, wouldn't that be nice to go and meet somebody and just sit and have that extra drink and overpriced eggs and all that kind of stuff? Just to sit and deep hang with somebody? The deep hang is what I miss."

Friendships come in funky, unusual containers. We can't possibly know what the future holds. The acquaintance whom I haven't spoken with in three years sent me a heartfelt card when my father-in-law passed away. The dear friend I assumed would be with me until we wore orthopedic footwear and drank mai tais by the pool in the retirement home hasn't returned my last four text messages.

Expectations are usually internal and unexpressed. But our behaviors express our expectations.

- Assuming a friend will be late to meet, so you take that into consideration when you make plans to get together
- Knowing your friend has small children, so you realize any effort on her part to recognize your birthday is a kind gesture

My friend Eve starts off every phone conversation with an apology. "I'm so sorry I haven't done a better job of keeping in touch," she'll say. "I suck as a friend." What I wish she'd understand is that I don't expect her to check in with me! I don't think of her as a bad friend because I've allowed the friendship to be what it is, which is one where we connect only when we can.

We must share our realistic expectations with our friends. In this context, realistic means that this is something you would reasonably reciprocate to your friend. It's not cool to expect your friend to drive across town to walk your dog for a week if you wouldn't offer the same. When you communicate your expectations, be specific.

- "It's important for me to hear from you on my birthday. It makes me feel good to hear your voice."

- "I would love it if we could exchange holidays gifts this year. How's $30 for a budget limit?"

- "The anniversary of my divorce is coming up. It would mean a lot if you checked in on me that day."

This might feel scary, but expressing your expectations is what a good teammate does.

Writer and podcast host Nina Badzin often sees these issues as the source of problems in friendships. Her listeners ask her for advice, which she shares on her show *Dear Nina: Conversations About Friendship*. What she sees as a common source of pain is that someone has made an assumption about a friend, and they are running with it and taking their feelings as fact. She also sees that lots of people chafe at being the default initiator, always texting or reaching out. "I wish I could point out that as long as the person says yes to your initiation of plans, or if they say no and they suggest another time, this isn't a problem. That is a friendship." All that matters at the end of the day is that your friend was responsive; it doesn't make sense to make a problem out of no problem, even though it could feel real to the friend going through it.

"So many people are not good at making plans," Badzin said. "And it's hard to accept." Some people are better at time management than others. Some people have a lot more friends to juggle, so they don't need to reach out to others as much, as they are always being sought out.

The answer to all these issues: TAKE OTHER PEOPLE'S BEHAVIORS LESS PERSONALLY. Instead of getting huffy, just let it be. "Because for whatever reason, that person just doesn't need plans," Badzin said. "Maybe they're more introverted and aren't interested in going out as much, but they're certainly happy to go out if someone asks. My point is, we don't know."

Stacy's Experience
Stacy wishes her friends didn't take her silence personally. She has a one-year-old son, and her life is chaotic. "I have no problem following up with a friend I haven't heard back from, sending an extra text, following up again, because I know it happens to me," she said.

"Sometimes I'll read a text and then go do something else. And I'm like, 'Oh my god. I totally forgot to answer.' I didn't even mean to do that." She hopes her friends give her lots of grace. "Definitely don't take my silence personally at all," she said.

NIX UNCERTAINTY

Uncertainty breeds anxiety. In her work with patients with social anxiety, Dr. Hendriksen often finds that they hesitate to reach out to a friend because they don't know how to do it correctly. They find this uncertainly paralyzing, as my dad learned when contemplating reaching out to his childhood friend.

"There's a sense of, *I need to do this well and say the exact right thing and send the exact right gift.* And so they end up not doing anything at all. It's all or nothing," she said. She'll hear from a client that their friend's parent died and they have no idea what's appropriate. Do they need to buy a card and write a heartfelt message? Do they need to find the perfect floral bouquet to send? "They've created fifteen steps for themselves. And so it's overwhelming and it's emotional, and they feel like they don't know what they're doing," Dr. Hendrickson said. "And so they just don't do anything."

As a consequence, the stalling friend feels horrible that they don't rise to the occasion. They know they botched the job and let their friend down. "But this sense of having to help and comfort correctly gets in the way," she said. "So I'm not making an excuse for those people, but I've seen the reason from the other side."

Stella's Experience

Stella told me she was the first one in her friend group who lost a parent. None of her friends knew how to act. Ironically enough, when her friend recently lost her dad, Stella was surprised that she had no idea how to act either. "I was trying not to do the things that really annoyed me that people did when my mom died. But then I found myself being like, I couldn't find the right words to say to her. She had a different relationship with her dad than I had with my mom."

The incident provided perspective. Maybe it's normal that people don't know how to act in these highly emotional situations.

To help our friends be there for us, we must minimize uncertainty. Anytime emotions are high and expectations are uncertain, give a realistic amount of information to your inner circle so they can show up with confidence.

Exercise: Be Explicit about What You Want

I. **The event:** Your cherished pet dies.

Minimize uncertainty to your friend: "I'm gutted over this loss. You don't have to send a card or flowers, but I would like to go out for a cup of coffee with you this week to lift my spirits."

Action item given to your friend: Schedule time to grab coffee with me.

Result: Your friend knows how to support you best.

II. **The event:** Your child's first birthday party.

Minimize uncertainty: "Hey! I would love to have you at the party, but I know children's birthday parties aren't really your thing. If you'd prefer, we can get together in the next week or two, just you and me. Maybe we can go for a long walk around your neighborhood. What do you think?"

Action item given to your friend: Schedule time to go for a walk together.

Result: Your friend knows they can decline the invitation to the kid's birthday party and your friendship is still strong and intact.

Now it's your turn to get creative in minimizing uncertainty.

III. **The event:** Your bachelorette party

Minimize uncertainty: "Hey! I'm excited to party with you at my bachelorette party. The party will take place on Saturday from 6 pm to 11 pm.

If you need to leave early for any reason, just know that's totally fine. I know you like working out early, so I get it! It's all good."

Action item given to your friend:

_____

Result:

_____

IV. **The event:** Caretaking for an older relative.

Minimize uncertainty:

_____

Action item given to your friend:

_____

Result:

_____

V. **The event:** You're quitting your job.

Minimize uncertainty:

_____

Action item given to your friend:

_____

Result:

_____

To be clear, laying out an action item is entirely optional. When you're grieving or under duress, it's not your job to explain to your friends how to comfort you, Dr. Hendriksen said. "At the same time, though, if someone wants to do that, what you can do is lower the expectations. Say, like, 'I just need a phone call. You don't have to say anything, you can you just listen. It would be helpful just to let me talk at you.'" If a person wants to give direction—which you do not have to do—it would create certainty. "You don't have to come up with some condolence speech. You can just breathe into the phone for half an hour. That's all I need.'"

By giving simple, realistic guidelines, you will be less likely to be disappointed by your friends' actions or nonactions. They will spend less mental energy guessing at your needs, which is a gift you give them. You're sending them a kind message in the huddle: "Hey, I don't expect you to know how to navigate this. Here's what I need."

TRY SOMETHING . . . ANYTHING!

If you're the one who doesn't know what your friend's expectations are, and you feel like you're stumbling in the dark, try *something*. When Dr. Hendriksen was in college, she wasn't sure what career she wanted to explore. Someone advised her to try any job. It didn't really matter because she would learn from it either way. If it's a good fit, great! If she hated it, at least she'd know what she didn't want to do.

Finding a way to relate to a friend in need involves taking a risk that you might get it wrong. The hope is that you will learn something about you and your friend either way. Go ahead and send that handwritten card or mail that care package. Don't fall into the trap of overthinking and talking yourself out of acknowledging your friends when they're in pain.

I've come up with little strategies so I don't have to reinvent the wheel. For instance, when a friend's pet passes away, I donate to an animal shelter in the pet's name. Or when a friend experiences a loss, I send a gift card to a meal delivery app. These aren't fancy things, but they take the guesswork out and show I care. That's a win/win, as business people say.

REALISTIC EXPECTATIONS ARE
INTEGRAL TO YOUR FRIENDSHIPS

So how do expectations tie in with friendships in adulthood? Well, I always thought once I had amazing, cherished friendships that our friendships would go on forever, as if they were on autopilot. I assumed my friendships would run in a parallel direction, just like a zipper. That's . . . not at all how any of this friendship thing works.

A lot of the issues that we have with romantic relationships also cross into friendship, said Natalie Lue, the host of the *The Baggage Reclaim Sessions* podcast and author of *The Joy of Saying No*. "Some people treat their friends like romantic partners or substitute siblings or substitute family," she said. There is this sense in friendships that one friend has to remain exactly the same as they were on the day when you first met. So if that friend changes, it feels like a rejection, like they're abandoning you, she said.

Social media has "helped" me keep in touch with my close friends in the same way a toddler offering to crack an egg for the cake you're making together "helps"—it just made a bigger mess and created more opportunity for mistakes.

The speed of modern communication screws with our expectations. "Texts have a lot to answer for in friendship tensions," Lue said. Because texting creates this expectation of instantaneous communication and unfettered access. We can see if our friend has read the message we sent. What Lue wants us to remember is that we all want to feel like we're super special. "But actually," she said, "what's happening is our text [to our friend] is coming through in the context of God knows how many other flippin' messages, texts, emails, whatever." We may not be privy to that information, so we focus on our needs not being met.

Resist filling in gaps of silence with anxiety and self-questioning. It's something you have to actively watch out for. You might hopscotch through thoughts like:

- What did I do wrong?
- This friend's got a problem with me.
- My friend is so rude.
- My friend doesn't value me or our friendship.

All of these thoughts from not receiving a text reply in a timely manner! "If you don't have that security in yourself, then it also manifests as insecurity in the friendship," Lue said. "And so then it feeds into this tension and you start to read things into it that aren't really there."

How busy can this friend possibly be? you might think. But all you need to know is that there are other priorities at the moment, and it's most likely not personal.

Lue reminds us to give ourselves and others grace too because we wouldn't want somebody saying, "Oh, she hasn't texted me back. She's got a problem with me."

I asked Kiaundra Jackson, a licensed marriage and family therapist, about the expectations we have for our friends. Our conversation made her reflect on her own friendships over the years, and how some of these friendships didn't have a strong, healthy connection; they were mostly just based on growing up together and knowing each other from going to the same church or attending the same school.

"But when you have choices and you get older, those relationships tend to change and you tend to gravitate to those friendships and those people that bring more value and more stability and more feedback," she said.[3] "That's going to just overall add value to your life." "And so I think the expectation that things are just supposed to stay the same is probably what we get wrong the most. And because we hold on to that idea so tightly when things shift and change, it's hard for us to reconcile or to realize that maybe this is a relationship that's no longer serving us, or the relationship has come to an end."[4]

Jackson fell into the same thinking that most of us probably have: *Yeah, my best friend and I are going to get older and life is going to happen. We may go our separate ways, but we'll always still stay connected. We'll still be tight. We'll travel and go see each other and talk on the phone. That connection will still be there.*

But her expectations didn't translate to reality. I truly wish we, as a society, were better prepared to weather these changes. Or at least get a heads-up that these changes are normal, expected, and inevitable.

"I don't think anyone has prepared us," Jackson said. "No one really talks about the relationship dynamics of how it will change when you grow and evolve and you get older."

In the face of these changes, she encourages us to accept these shifts because a friendship appearing stalled feels identical to a friendship that is dead. "Sometimes it's hard to decipher the two when you've been connected with someone for so long. But sometimes we have to figure out, like, 'Hey, is this life just life-ing,' and this person is going through life and changes and setbacks . . . and that's just how they are navigating their relationships right now with more distance. Or is this relationship just completely over and I've been holding on to it for too long and now it's time to come to grips where it's like, 'I need to just let it go'"?

If you truly aren't sure if your friendship is paused or ended, you can always attempt to get rid of uncertainty. Ask your friend outright: Is our friendship on the back burner at the moment, or has it run its course? See what they say, then watch their actions. If your friend has been nonresponsive or refuses to give you an answer about the status of your friendship, assume the friendship is over. Functional friendships are reciprocal. If yours is not, then you aren't in a functional friendship. If there's no hard feelings on either side, be open to the door reopening at some point when circumstances change.

TWO MOUNTAINS, TWO EXPERIENCES

Why do people want to climb Mount Everest? My guess is that part of the allure of scaling Everest (for some) is the social currency of saying you've climbed our planet's highest mountain. People want to display that photo of themselves grinning at the summit on their desk or over their fireplace mantel. They want that riveting story about how scary nature is (avalanches!) or how rickety their equipment proved to be (faulty oxygen sensors!). They want to impress their friends and colleagues over a neat tumbler of Pappy Van Winkle bourbon (or a peanut butter chia seed protein shake? I have no idea what modern-day adventurers eat or drink when regaling people with their mountaineering stories).

In reality, climbing Mount Everest today is—excuse my French—a shit show. Due to the influx of trekkers, the mountain is littered with junk. Food waste, bathroom waste, spent oxygen tanks, soiled clothing, damaged equipment—it's like the aftermath of Woodstock '99 in the Himalayas.

The average Everest trekker is estimated to create eighteen pounds of trash during their climb. This is a problem because *checks notes* there are no trash collectors on the mountain.

The out-of-control garbage situation has become so dire that some experts have called for a pause on climbing Everest altogether. A slowdown will give the area a fighting chance to recover from the ecological nightmare that tourists bring to the vulnerable, fragile location.

The problem? Too many people are making too much money off of the Everest experience to allow a slowdown. The local economy in Nepal is dependent on the tourism the mountain brings.

The ideal season to climb the mountain is short—May gives the best chance of experiencing favorable weather for an ascent—which only increases the pressure to make as much money off the tourists as possible within the small seasonal window. Government officials issue pricey permits to foreigners interested in the climb, so they're not keen to tighten restrictions, which would impact their bottom line.

Conservationists say it's kinder to the environment for mountaineers to find local peaks to climb. This would significantly reduce the hefty carbon footprint of taking long plane rides and car trips to the remote mountain area.

Mountain climbing, as a sport (calling? hobby?) is actually a recent-ish invention. For most of time immemorial, people were happy to let mountains be, well, giant heaps of rock in the distance.

It wasn't until the mid-nineteenth century that people didn't just want to admire mountains, they wanted to ascend them. "Looking at mountains? Lame. Painting mountains? BORING. Climbing a mountain and feeling like I'm king of the world? *Tell me more*," say nineteenth-century Europeans, leaning in and cocking an eyebrow.

Sir Edmund Hillary, an explorer from New Zealand, along with Nepali-Indian Sherpa mountaineer Tenzing Norgay, were the first pair to summit Everest in 1953. Since then, almost 12,000 people have ascended the mountain, according to the Himalayan Database, a nonprofit organization keeping track of Everest's stats. Hundreds of people have died attempting Everest on both routes on the Chinese and Nepalese sides of the mountain.

If the challenge of the twentieth century was figuring out how to give the mountaineering experience to anyone who can afford it—regardless of their experience or physical fitness—the challenge of the twenty-first century is how can one experience this feeling of ascending a mountain in a way that doesn't put the environment (and, hello, their LIFE!) at risk?

What if we couldn't climb Mount Everest anymore? Is there any other way to fully appreciate the mountain's beauty without placing boots on the summit?

Australia's Uluru (formerly known as Ayers Rock) has faced this conundrum. As the world's largest monolith, it too became a modern attraction for international tourists to ascend. This arkosic sandstone rock is a tor, an isolated mass of weathered rock, and it's roughly half a billion years old. The mound, which is 2,831 feet high and roughly six miles around, is sacred to indigenous Aboriginal Australians.

In the late 1940s, visitors began efforts to climb the rock, according to the Uluru-Kata Tjuta National Park website.[5] By the 1970s, the Australian government saw some of the same problems appear that plague the Nepalese with Everest: larger groups of tourists mean more trash, more crowds, and more devastation to the local environment.

In 1985, the Australian government returned ownership of Uluru to the local Pitjantjatjara people. One of the conditions of the handover was that the Aboriginal people would lease the park back to the National Parks and Wildlife agency for ninety-nine years. Furthermore, the land would be jointly managed between them.

On November 1, 2017, the Uluru-Kata Tjuta National Park board voted unanimously to prohibit the public from climbing Uluru.[6] The ban took effect in the fall of 2019. In lieu of climbing, park officials encourage visitors to appreciate the natural beauty of the rock formation and local flora and fauna on foot. Not only is this approach more respectful to the environment, it's respectful to the native people who feel a deep connection to the land.

Everest embodies one challenge: pursuing a desired outcome at whatever financial, physical, and environmental cost to do it. Uluru embodies another challenge: how to appreciate nature without feeling the need to dominate it. Two mountains, two experiences.

Everest as a rigid experience

- Dominating: Conquering the harsh conditions

- Rigid: There are only a few narrow ways to ascend the mountain

- Black-or-white thinking: You either summit or you don't

Uluru as a flexible experience

- Open: Being in harmony with the fragile natural conditions

- Respectful: Understanding that there are lots of ways to marvel at the mountain's natural beauty

- Flexible: Being willing to take in a mountain's majesty without having one particular experience

This mountain example is a metaphor for the challenges we face in our modern friendships. If you decide a friendship is your Everest, you're going to heap too much trash on it in your attempt to dominate the mountain and bend elements to your will. Yet, if you consider your friendship mountain as sacred, you will find a way to honor the friendship in a constantly evolving, respectful way. You'll consider the totality of the environment you're in and working with limits instead of clashing against them. Yes, we might have more family and work obligations and less leisure time than in the past, but it's not like our social life is over; it just looks different. Problems in adulthood are more complex, so they need more nuanced, sensitive solutions. Remember, as long as the desire for a friendship is present, anything is possible!

MAKE SMALL TWEAKS

In 2022, an Irish deejay named Annie Macmanus had a brilliant idea to throw a raging dance party that concluded at a reasonable hour. Journalist Anna Codrea-Rado reported on the event for the *New York Times*.[7] Macmanus—aka Annie Mac—calls the party "Before Midnight," and it takes place at a 2,000-person capacity nightclub in London. Festivities start at 7 pm and end at midnight. It provides all the wild fun of a night out but none of the late nights, which is perfect for fellow parents and worker bees, Codrea-Rado reported.

"Nightclubbing is not designed for people who need sleep," Macmanus wrote on an Instagram post explaining her vision for the party. "So I'm shifting the time parameters forwards, and bringing you a fully authentic clubbing experience that starts at 7 pm and ends at the strike [*sic*] of midnight."

This party, she said, is designed for those "who need to be sharp and useful at the weekends and just can't afford sleepless nights." Before Midnight has been a smashing success. That one little tweak, shifting the time frame of the dance party, opened up an entire universe of fun.

Macmanus challenged a long-held tenet of clubbing: that events had to start at 9 pm or 10 pm and run until the wee hours of the night. By offering an earlier runtime, the event appealed to an entirely new audience who thought their dancing days were in the rearview mirror.

"This wasn't just a story about a fun club night; it was about how one small tweak, a change in the schedule, can make a joyous, wonderful difference in people's lives," Codrea-Rado wrote in her newsletter, talking about the process of reporting the piece.[8]

Small tweaks in your friendship could look like:

- Meeting earlier or at different times than usual

- Sending voice memos instead of text messages

- Coming up with new rules for gift exchanges: "We only exchange chocolate snacks we can share immediately with each other upon unwrapping"

- Imagining new rules for places to eat: only places with vegetarian options under $20. Or places within a ten-minute driving distance

- Not centering your hangouts around drinking

It's on us to be creative about how to carve out time and space for connection. But it's not your imagination—our options for finding places to get together outside of work or home can be limited. These "third places" offer a respite from our routines and household drudgery. The bar in *Cheers* is a third place. So is Central Perk in *Friends*. *Saved By the Bell* had The Max, and *Beverly Hills, 90210* had the Peach Pit.

Part of the problem modern friendships may face is that third places are harder to come by. These third places allow us to spend massive amounts of time together. Think of them like a friendship incubator. It's where you can share your troubles and make each other laugh.

Dr. Hall agrees that the decline of central meeting places takes a toll on our social lives. "Part of the challenge is there's no shared space," he said. What's increasingly become the third place for people is their smartphones. That's a problem because smartphones are not a replacement for in-person interactions.

In a 2017 study published in the *Journal of Experimental Sociology*, researchers Mahdi Roghanizad of Western University and Vanessa Bohns of Cornell University found that people tend to overestimate the power of their persuasiveness in text or email and underestimate the power of their persuasiveness in face-to-face communication.[9] How massive of a difference? "Face-to-face requests were 34 times more effective than emailed ones," Bohns reported in the *Harvard Business Review*.[10]

The biggest downside to email is its absence nonverbal cues that generate trust and empathy, the study said. Requests made over email were easier to blow off. However, since people generally don't like letting others down, requests made face-to-face had a much higher success rate.

"The alternatives to face-to-face communication are more than they have ever been," Dr. Hall said. One of the paradoxes he thinks about is that even though we have more options than ever for keeping in touch with friends, people aren't using these channels to communicate with each other.

Part of the reason is that there's less work and less reward to texts and emails. Put simply: it's less effort to send a message than to schedule a phone call or a hangout. "People are actually looking for the least common denominator," Dr. Hall said. "So if they feel like they actually are connecting in some way through a group chat, or through a social media app or through a text, then they're like, 'Well, that's it. I've already done my thing.'"

But his research says that talking over the phone and being together in person are not the same. It's not comparable to the in-person hangout. The problem is that organizing get-togethers takes way more effort as opposed to liking a picture on a social media site.

Given that, we have to be choosy, practical, and realistic when it comes to expending our limited resources of energy, time, and attention. You cannot be the same level of friend to everyone you've met in your life. That would be problematic if you held yourself to that impossible standard. You must zero in on a few meaningful bonds that you can realistically invest in.

Marley's Experience

"I keep few close friends, and I nurture these relationships like one might water plants," Marley tells me. "I tend to them daily. For instance, my friend Liza lives in Montana, but I text her daily, just to say I'm thinking of her or to tell her I love her. My bestie Amy and I make each other laugh and meet up at least twice a month to do something we both enjoy. And my soul sister Poppy and I can always go deep, sharing our most tender vulnerabilities in a way that promotes self-reflection and growth."

These are the people in Marley's Jacuzzi. These are the people she prioritizes. Make small tweaks with a select number of friends. Adapting to each other's life changes gives your friendship a better chance to survive in the long term.

Speaking of friendships that span the ages, one of the most important aspects of friendship is learning how to be authentic with one another. That starts with learning how to decline invitations gracefully, which I'll teach you in the next chapter.

14

How to Say No Without Crumpling into a Ball of Self-Hatred

"Do you want to go to a polka festival with me?" No offense to any polka-heads out there, but this does not sound fun to me because I'm a crotchety old house cat easily spooked by crowds and loud noises. It's sweet that a friend would ask me to go with her, I guess, but I really don't want to spend an afternoon being jostled by rambunctious polka fans. That's a no from me, Dawg.

Sometimes a friend will extend an invitation that you will want to decline. The people pleaser in you might feel uncomfortable with that. In fact, you might convince yourself that it's easier to say yes to things you don't want to do in order to avoid disappointing your friend.

I asked author and recovered people pleaser Natalie Lue what is the most empowering advice she would give to people pleasers. "*No* is not a dirty word," she said. "*Yes* is really the inverse of no, so we don't have to get so hung up on this idea that no is a bad thing. When you say yes to something, you're saying no to something else. And when you say no to something, you're saying yes to something else." There's a yin and a yang going on here.

Lue thinks that previous painful experiences of friendship contribute to why somebody feels uncomfortable being themselves. "They're afraid of being judged," she said. "They're afraid that if they don't say that they like all the same things, that they want to do all the same things, if they don't act like they think that the other person wants them to, then the other person is not going to want to have this relationship with them."

Veronica's Experience

"I have a visceral reaction when people try to claim my time," Veronica told me. Her mom passed away last year, and Veronica noticed that one friend of hers has been pushier about the two hanging out. This friend proposes coffee dates and going out dancing. She texts her all the time: *When are you free? What are you doing?* Veronica felt pressured and was disappointed that the dynamic of their friendship has changed.

"I don't know if it's the pandemic. I don't know if my friend is trying to be supportive because my mom died. I don't know if she just changed and she wants more out of this friendship. For whatever reason, it makes me feel stuck and claustrophobic," Veronica said.

Here, Veronica doesn't know how to turn down a friend asking for more connection. It can feel sticky. Especially if you know your friend doesn't respond well to being told no. There are a few things you can do in these instances:

Ask for clarification, if you need it. "Are you asking me to brunch, lunch, or dinner?"

Be polite. Acknowledge the invitation. Thank them for it.

Ask for time. Say, "Let me think about it" before reflexively saying yes.

Decline. Say, "Thank you for thinking of me, but I cannot attend."

Or renegotiate with something you would be willing to do. Suggest another time or another activity instead.

Friend #1: Would you like to go to a baseball game with me?
Friend #2: (being authentic) "Thanks for thinking of me, but baseball's not my thing. Would you want to go to a movie instead?"

Friend #1: Want to grab a drink sometime?
Friend #2: (being authentic) "Thanks for the invite, but I'm not drinking these days. Would you want to go on a picnic instead? I can bring fancy seltzers."

Exercise: Turn Down Plans

Now it's your turn to decline plans. Write down how you'd respond:

Friend: "Want to watch the new Dane Cook comedy special with me?"

Your authentic answer:

_____

Friend: "Want to go eat at LOLJK, that new raw vegetable restaurant across town? It costs $200 a head, and they only serve celery and radishes."

Your authentic answer:

_____

Friend: "Want to go to the Eminem look-alike contest? My baby cousin is a contestant."

Your authentic answer:

_____

HOW TO DECLINE FAVORS

This is another pain point for all of us people pleasers. Your friends will ask you for help from time to time. If you can do it, great. If you can't, it can feel stressful to decline to help, especially if you're a people pleaser. Disappointing friends often feels excruciating, but interestingly, you may find that it's easier to say no to some friends than to others. Usually it's the friendships that feel the most tenuous or fraught that can trigger your sense of worry.

This is why knowing your priorities is key. We can't agree to favors for everyone who asks. You'd run yourself ragged. That's not sustainable.

As a wholehearted friend, there are only certain tiers of people you consider doing big favors for: your Jacuzzi friends. Swimming pool friends are heavily considered, but their requests are going to require more careful deliberation.

1. Ask for clarification if needed. Understand exactly what your friend is asking you to do.

2. Gauge when they need an answer. Your friend needs to know if you can help or not so they can make other arrangements if needed.

3. Explain what you are willing to do. Set a boundary in a way you feel good about. Honor your other commitments.

Friend #1: "Can you help me move next weekend?"
Friend #2: "Unfortunately, I already have plans next weekend with my in-laws. I'm happy to help you pack on Thursday. And I can help you unpack on Monday afternoon. If my plans change, I'll let you know."

Friend #1: "Can you help me prepare for this job interview?"
Friend #2: "I'm not available at the moment because I'm slammed at work. I can call you on my lunch break if there's something you want to run past me. Are you free at 12:30 pm?"

Friend #1: "Can you cat sit for me next week? I need you to feed Fluffy from Monday through Saturday."

Friend #2: "I can help two of the days, preferably Monday and Tuesday. Let me know if you can find coverage the rest of the time. If you can't, I can help you look for local cat sitters."

Friend #1: "Can you watch my kids on Thursday?"
Friend #2: "I can't this Thursday. I'm free on Wednesday if you can move your appointment."

By the way, you don't always need an unimpeachable reason to refuse plans with a friend. Barring an emergency on your friend's part, resting and spending time by yourself are plans you should keep because you are the one who suffers the most when overextended. Feel free to say no to last-minute hangout requests, expensive destination weddings, and anything in between, even if you don't have a pressing reason to decline. "No" is a complete sentence, as they say. A wholehearted friend communicates to a friend whether or not they can accept an invitation or extend a favor in a timely manner; it's your friend's responsibility to manage any disappointment or sadness on their end.

Before I prioritized being authentic with my needs and availability, I would say yes to anything my friends asked me to do, even if I didn't feel like it. Late-night dinners at too-expensive restaurants, staying for "one more" glass of wine even though I was ready to head home, catsitting for the week between Christmas and New Year's. To be honest, I liked being included, and I felt that if I didn't agree to hang out with my friend or say yes to their request, then the invitations would stop coming. This wasn't a stellar strategy because I'd secretly resent friends for bothering me. Couldn't they understand that my preferred natural state is lying horizontal with my iPad balanced on my chest? People kept making me do things! Getting in my car. Putting on pants. Wearing a bra (not in that order).

My inability to say no has been my version of Aladdin's magic carpet: It has shown me the world! It's taken me to:

- Going to a warehouse party in West Philly because my friend had a crush on some dude who said he'd be there

- Eating a seafood tower in Las Vegas that I couldn't afford

- Playing a round of miniature golf in Orlando, Florida

- Sitting front row at an open-mic poetry slam in San Diego

My friendships felt like hostage situations, but with more tinted lip gloss and low-stakes local gossip. Saying yes to things I really didn't want to do put a lot of pressure on me. We didn't feel on equal footing. It also wasn't fair to my friends. I wasn't being honest with them. Being inauthentic took its toll on these friendships.

We want to sidestep this destructive habit and nip this people-pleasing crap in the bud. Wholehearted friends strive to be authentic with their needs and availability. It's a commitment you make to yourself so that your friends will know you—and your limits—better.

The fact of the matter is, if you have no boundaries, you won't have true intimacy. "If you never say no to your friends or to your family or to your partner, you are not being honest with them," Lue said. "They don't know you. They don't know where they stand." When you start being authentic, relationships will fit you better. People will know where they stand with you, which will help you feel better about yourself. "That's empowering and it's liberating," Lue said. "I'm saying no [to things I don't want to do], but I'm also saying yes to intimacy. I'm saying yes to having a better relationship with my partner and my friends."

"Nobody wants to be with a 'yes' person," she added. "Once I reached that stage in my life where I became a recovering people pleaser and I became more myself, a lot of the old anxieties or frictions just dropped off because there was a safety within all those friendships that I had." Wholehearted friendships are all about this psychological safety. That's the goal with these tweaks: tailoring your behaviors so your friendships will fit you better.

Now that we know the elements of Wholehearted Friendship, in part 3, we'll begin the fun process of putting this knowledge into practice. I will teach you how to be the kind of friend people will cherish, how to organize exciting hangouts, how to express gratitude, and how to be a caring person whom people cherish and respect. Part 3 is a how-to manual for being a terrific teammate to the most awesome people in your life. Let's goooooo!

PART 3

PRACTICING WHOLEHEARTED FRIENDSHIP

15

Let's (Actually) Get Together Sometime

Okay, igniters out there. It's game time. We're putting the pedal to the metal, so to speak, and we're reaching out to our friends. It's exciting, I agree. Real quick: When coming up with these exercises, I was inspired by the structure in the book *How to Talk So Kids Will Listen & Listen So Kids Will Talk*. I just wanted to give the authors a shout-out and credit them for their brilliance as I designed these exercises.

STEP 1: FRAME THE INVITATION SO YOUR FRIEND CAN SAY YES

Before most happy memories happen, an invitation is extended in a way people can say yes to. Over crab chowder, Amelia Earhart probably didn't say, "Want to hop on a plane together sometime?" No. She probably said, "Want to go for a quick jaunt together *now* while we're wearing gowns and gloves." She was specific about the ask so Eleanor Roosevelt could say yes!

Think about the way you extend invitations to people in your life. Look at the difference it makes when you are more specific. Which of these text messages would you be more delighted to receive? Circle the one you'd be more likely to get jazzed about.

I. Good: "Hey! We should get together sometime."

Better: "Want to get manicures with me sometime?"

Best: "Want to get manicures next weekend? I'm thinking 11 am on Saturday at the place near your gym. We can grab Chipotle afterwards if you have time."

II. Good: "Thinking of you!"

Better: "Thinking of you! Any interest in going to a farmers market with me sometime soon?"

Best: "Thinking of you! Any interest in going to a farmers market with me on Saturday from 10am to noon? We can grab almond croissants from the new bakery that just opened nearby."

III. Good: "Thinking of you."

Better: "Thinking of you. I know you had a busy week at work."

Best: "Thinking of you. I know you had a monstrously busy week. I figured you would be too busy to want to cook dinner. Let me order you a pizza from Rizzo's. My treat. Text me your order and I'll call it in. Love you!"

IV. Good: "It's been too long since we've seen each other."

Better: "It's been too long since we've seen each other. Any interest in going with me to that new tapas place? Their sangria looks amazing."

Best: "It's been too long since we've seen each other. Any interest in going with me to the new tapas place for sangria on Thursday? Say, 6 pm? We need sangria in our lives."

Exercise

Now you try.

V. Good: "How have you been?"

Better:

_____

Best:

_____

VI. Good: "Are you around?"

Better:

_____

Best:

_____

VII. Good: "Hey friend! I miss you!"

Better:

_____

Best:

_____

STEP 2: MAKE SILENCES MEAN SOMETHING

One trick I've learned as a journalist is to explain how I will interpret a silence. This is a gift to both participants in any email or text conversation. I've let the other person know that their noncommunication is now coded as communication to me.

For instance, when I pitch a story to an editor, I'll say: "If I don't hear from you by Friday [or whenever], I'll assume it's a pass. I'll be in touch soon with another idea." This sentence releases me from refreshing my inbox nonstop. I've started doing this with my friends now.

- If I don't hear back from you by 10 am, I'll assume you're not available for brunch. I'll reach out again next week.

- If I don't hear back by 3 pm about whether you can help me move, I'll assume you're not available. I'll ask some other friends to see if they can do it.

- If you don't hear back from me by Friday at noon about getting coffee this weekend, assume I can't do it. I'll ping you next week to reschedule.

- If I don't get back to you about signing up for that yoga class by Monday night, go ahead and take the class without me.

- If I don't hear back from you by the end of the day about which days you can go on vacation with me, I'll assume you can't make the trip. I'll make the reservations without you. You can always join me later on if you are able to make it!

Exercise

Now you try. Make the silences mean something.

Asking a friend if they want to join me to watch a movie:

_____

Asking a friend if they want to go on a trip with me:

_____

Asking a friend if they want to go for a walk with me:

_____

Once you realize you can make silences mean something when you attach a deadline, then you liberate both people from being held hostage waiting for a response.

<hr>

STEP 3: TRY NOT TO TAKE REJECTION PERSONALLY

Friends are going to throw a lot of shit at you. They come with their own emotions, traumas, obsessions, needs, and desires. You cannot know all of them. But you can minimize points of friction. Humans are genetically suited to exist in a community. It's in our DNA.

When a loss or threat to our social relationships occurs, the exclusion can feel physically painful. In 2011, University of Michigan social psychologist Ethan Kross coauthored a study published in the *Proceedings of the National Academy of Sciences* that established how rejection and physical pain are similar.[1] Researchers showed forty people who recently underwent an unwanted break up a photograph of their ex-partner. Then they asked the subjects to think about being rejected. The areas of the brain that support the sensory components of physical pain (the secondary somatosensory cortex and dorsal posterior insula) lit up like a Christmas tree. The study showed that not only are social exclusion and physical pain both distressing to experience, but they also share a common somatosensory representation as well. The pathways are intertwined.

In an online survey I circulated while doing research for this book, the number one thing most people wished for was that their friends reached out to them more. We *ache* for our friends to need us. We want them to initiate with us, to include us in their lives. But sometimes your efforts to get together with your friends will be frustrating. It won't gel in the way you'd hoped.

Gabe's Experience

After college, Gabe was living in the UK, and he felt like he had enough friends. Then, he had one close friendship fall apart. This was painful to him because he's had this circle of friends since the fourth grade. They felt like family to him. "If I met them now, I might not choose them. But they are who I'm stuck with," he told me. He can't wrap his head around how to add new friends to the rotation.

He worked out at the gym with a few guys for a couple of months, then that faded. "I wish I had more answers," he said. "I wish I were a friendship influencer to be like, 'Play tennis.' But, I don't have it in me. I'm not that kind of social person. For me, it's all vibes-based. Like, I'm not going to join a league or whatever. I just don't think that would work for me," he said. "I hate to be so cliché, but it's a time and a money thing."

It can be hard to accept that some people are better at time management than you are. Some people have a lot more friends than you do, so their free time is more limited. "And so for whatever it is, they don't need to reach out as much as they are always being reached out to," Ms. Badzin said. "That's the way it goes." People's capacity for socialization is different. Try not to get discouraged if it takes time to find and build your community. Your job right now is to plant seeds and see which ones sprout.

In the next chapter, we'll explore how to express appreciation and support in a wholehearted way. For anyone who's tripped over their words when consoling a friend, relax. This next chapter is for you!

16

Expressing Appreciation and Support the Right Way

We've identified who matters to us and what vital roles our Jacuzzi and swimming pool friends play. We understand that friendships need a clear and compelling reason to feel fulfilling. At this point, you're igniting all over the place, asking friends to get together for reasons that excite you both. You've been authentic with your needs and availability. And you've noticed what's going on in your friends' lives. Go, you!!

Now you're sitting in the Mexican restaurant with your buddy nibbling on chips and guacamole. This is the main event. You've identified the clear and compelling reason that brought you to this spot. You reached out and made these plans happen. So far, so good. You're positioning yourself for the in-person Maximum Friend Experience (MFE). The challenge: How do you communicate to this friend in a way that makes them feel seen, heard, cared for, and supported while spending time together?

You aren't just any old friend anymore; you're learning how to be a wholehearted friend, one who practices Dr. Glasser's seven habits of connection:

1. Supporting

2. Encouraging

3. Listening

4. Accepting

5. Trusting

6. Respecting

7. Negotiating differences

We demonstrate these behaviors by:

- Expressing appreciation and gratitude

- Being a caring and curious person

- Providing comfort

- Offering effective help

- Respectfully giving advice

I will walk you through how to do these things with sensitivity and integrity. This will let your friends know that they matter to you. They will feel nurtured and loved. The small, simple behavioral tweaks I suggest will transform how you relate to others—and how your friends relate to you. Friends will be more trusting toward you because they know you won't judge them. They will seek you out because you don't try to dominate them or bombard them with unsolicited advice. You, and your friendship, will be a safe haven. Both people will feel seen, heard, and respected. Your friendships will be everything you want and need them to be.

Exercise: Express Appreciation

To make your friend feel appreciated, describe how your friend's behavior makes you feel.

When you pick up my calls, it makes me feel:

_____

When you listen to my rants, it makes me feel:

_____

When you remember my birthday, it makes me feel:

_____

When you spend time running errands with me, it makes me feel:

_____

When you bring me little gifts, it makes me feel:

_____

When you text me randomly to make me laugh, it makes me feel:

_____

When you reach out to ask me how my day is going, it makes me feel:

_____

When you support my career and celebrate my accomplishments, it makes me feel:

_____

Having you as my friend makes me feel:

_____

These expressions are so simple, but it's such an effective way to make your friend feel appreciated.

HOW TO SHOW GRATITUDE: GIVE A MEMORABLE COMPLIMENT

Compliments are a gift, albeit one that can feel challenging to accept. Many people are terrible at receiving compliments. We're experts at deflecting, minimizing, or outright rejecting compliments in an attempt to resist feelings of superiority. ("I love your new haircut!" "Eh, it's too choppy. I hate it.")

There are plenty of reasons why someone might eschew accolades. It can be stressful to feel like people notice whether you're doing something well or not. But it's worth pushing through the discomfort and learning how to accept a compliment gracefully—and gratefully—because you'll be able to reap a host of health benefits. Authentic praise can help you learn new skills and behaviors. Participants who received a compliment while learning a new song on a piano were more likely to recall how to play the song in the long term. Turns out, the brain releases dopamine when we receive approval.[1] This neurotransmitter is linked with wanting pleasure, and increasing motivation, focus, and positivity.

Paying someone a compliment can also improve your life in a different way. You see, praise activates the same areas in the brain that light up when one receives rewards like money or romantic attention (the ventral striatum and the ventral medial prefrontal cortex, FYI). If you want to reinforce positive behavior in a friend, offer them a sincere compliment. It'll make it more likely they will repeat the desired behavior in the future.

Social media is compliment culture on full display, where we bestow "likes" on others and tally the ones we get ourselves. However, that can be tricky, as tone doesn't always translate well on social media. With that in mind, here's how to give and receive a meaningful compliment, both online and IRL, so everyone walks away feeling great.

Before you give a compliment
1. **Slow down.** Something that may *appear* praiseworthy may in fact be a sensitive issue. For instance, you might compliment a friend on her svelte figure although she's secretly battling an illness and is struggling to maintain weight. This misstep can happen in the virtual world too. If you're about to chime in with praise online, make sure you've actually read the caption accompanying the post. Allow yourself enough time to glance over the comment, and think twice about what you're saying.

2. **Know your intentions.** If you're tossing out compliments like Oprah Winfrey (You get a compliment! And you get a compliment!), take a step back. If you're attempting to foster a connection with someone you admire, or operating out of a desire to be popular, hold off. Be clear about what you're trying to gain with these compliments, and then reevaluate if this is the best way to achieve that.

3. **Discern what should be posted publicly.** And what should be shared privately. Generally speaking, when people post an accomplishment publicly, it's fine for us to comment with praise publicly.

When giving a compliment

1. **Be precise.** Rather than saying, "Beautiful!" to a friend in a lovely sweater, it's better for you to be specific and say, "That color is really flattering on you." If you're complimenting someone you work with, home in on a particular attribute of your colleague. Something like: "I can tell you put a lot of effort into this project. The charts you developed helped me understand the situation much better." The more you zero in on a particular element, the more credible your compliment will be.

2. **Elaborate.** If you're posting a comment online, do more than popping in a heart emoji. Spend a few moments brainstorming a thoughtful, funny, or valuable comment. You'll likely capture the attention of the recipient, as well as other people scrolling by. However, don't go overboard here. If you drone on and on about how much you admire or enjoy something, it might come off as insincere. Balance is key!

3. **Avoid bringing yourself into it.** One common mistake people make is using a compliment to compare achievements. "Oh, you got a raise? I just earned a raise too." Keep the focus on the person who has earned the praise.

After you've received a compliment

1. **Say thank you.** Feel free to acknowledge compliments the same way they were given. So if someone mails you a gift, then you would mail them a thank-you card. Similarly, if someone compliments you with a full-blown sentence on your social media post, then it would be most appropriate to respond in the same manner. If you need training wheels and need to reply with *something*, say a few filler words like "Oh, that's so thoughtful of you," or "You're very kind."

2. **Be gracious.** If you're overwhelmed with compliments on social media—say, the pic you posted of your engagement ring is blowing up, and everyone from your neighbor to your third cousin is chiming in with well wishes—it's perfectly acceptable to post a blanket thank-you sentiment to everyone who left nice comments. Something like: "Thank you, everyone, for your kind words."

   If you aren't able to spend energy attending to every comment or want to limit future updates to those in your inner circle, only share your updates with people whose opinions really matter to you.

3. **Avoid returning a compliment out of nervousness.** When someone gives you a compliment, you may be tempted to return the favor out of anxiety. Resist the urge, people! A better response to a compliment is to ask the person a question pinpointing what they liked about the thing you did. This is a constructive way to keep the conversation on the topic without shifting the attention to the other person out of discomfort.

"I loved your speech."

"Thank you. What part did you connect with most?"

"Your kids are so well behaved."

"Thanks! What did you notice about their behavior?"

"That ring is to die for."

"Thank you! What about it caught your eye?"

"I inhaled that cake you made. You are a wonderful baker."

"Thank you! Are you interested in baking too?"

4. **Share the glow.** Give credit where credit is due. If someone praises your bonkers-amazing houseplant collection, spread the love and say, "Thank you! My friend Stephanie taught me everything about tending plants." In fact, by sharing praise and acknowledging others who have contributed to your success, you're showing your friends that their support matters to you.

HOW TO SHOW GRATITUDE: GIFT GIVING

It's so easy to go wrong with giving gifts to our friends. Just like advice and compliments, giving gifts can be a sensitive area. Outwardly, we probably think we prioritize the gift recipient's wants and needs when choosing a gift for them. But researchers find that the process doesn't exactly go down like that.

Most people want to give an over-the-top, wow-worthy gift that will surprise and delight the recipient. You want them to be blown away by your thoughtfulness and innovation. A 2018 study by marketing professors Adelle X. Yang and Oleg Urminsky published in *Psychological Science* found, confirmed this.[2] They found that people tend to focus on what they call the smile-seeking motive. Here, gift givers may choose to forgo "satisfaction-maximizing gifts" (something versatile and useful to own) and instead favor giving "reaction-maximizing gifts" (something that will elicit a winning-a-new-car on *The Price Is Right* freakout).

Gifting a friend a pair of tickets to Coachella could say *I want to feel closeness with you so let's go this event together*. Ignoring a friend's wedding registry and commissioning a piece of custom artwork for the newlyweds could send the message *Registries are for chumps. In fact, I know you better than you know yourself so I had this made special for you.*

It's not bad to want to send a message through your gift. Often, the messages are benign. But make sure that the message you're sending with the gift you select is in fact the message you'd like to send. When it comes to gifts, there are three entities: the giver, the receiver, and the context of the exchange—is the gift out of obligation or not?

Obligatory gifts are the ones we give because we're fulfilling an expectation (a secret Santa exchange at work, birthday presents, housewarming gifts, etc.). Voluntary gifts are given with no expectations attached to them (baking a "welcome to the neighborhood" loaf of banana bread for a new neighbor, giving a $15 Starbucks gift card to your coworker to thank them for their help on a project).

When it comes to gift giving, we should focus on what our friends enjoy instead of what we selfishly prefer that our friends enjoy. This could look like gifting a pricey bottle of gin to a diehard whiskey drinker because you want your friend to experience your favorite spirit. Don't be surprised if you notice the gin bottle tucked away at the back of the cabinet the next time you go to their house.

When giving gifts, keep these thoughts in mind:

- Gift receivers often prefer to own gifts that are practical, versatile, and useful.

- If you're stuck on what to give a friend, ask them! Surprise is overrated. Give your friend a chance to express their expectations so you can meet them.

- If you're stuck, think of what is important to your friend and let that lead you. For instance, for one holiday, I ordered custom mugs with drawings of my friends and their pets on them. They were a hit! I thought, *What do my friends love? Their pets!* And I let that thought guide me.

- When in doubt, go sentimental. Frame a photo of the two of you. Write a handwritten card. You can never tell your friends how much you love and appreciate them enough!

Expressing appreciation for your friends is a fantastic way to help them feel seen, heard, and valued. The essential thing is to keep their needs, wants, and preferences at the forefront. The great thing about gifts is that if you don't blow anyone's socks off, there are always more opportunities to fine-tune your gifting styles down the road.

Now that we have the complimentary words and actions ironed out, let's go deeper into the moves you can make to really show your friends you care for them.

17

How to Be Caring and Curious

On an episode of the comedy podcast *SmartLess*, the three hosts—Jason Bateman, Will Arnett, and Sean Hayes—discussed their guest, actor Justin Theroux.[1] This widow-peaked former boyfriend of Jennifer Aniston not only looks smokin' hot in a pair of thin sweatpants (seriously, Google it), but apparently, he's also a superman of a friend. Listen to the way the hosts talk about him:

Sean Hayes: He's a great guy. I don't know him, like I said, as well as you guys. He's so down-to-earth and like somebody you immediately want to get to know and hang out with.
Will Arnett: He's very real. He's such a—
Jason Bateman: His wit is so fast.
Will Arnett: He's so fast. He's so smart. He's so funny. And he's so sweet. He's such a sweet guy, and he's been an unbelievable friend over the years in every way. He's one of those guys who's super loyal. He's the guy you can call at any time. It doesn't matter, he'll be the first guy there. And Jason would be the last.
Jason Bateman: Well, you need bookends.

Real. Smart. Funny. Sweet. Loyal. I mean, who wouldn't want their friends to describe them this way? Isn't that what we *all* want, to have our friends appreciate us? For our friends to know how much we treasure them *and* for them to see our effort? This is like, the holy grail of friendship.

When Will Arnett talks about what impresses him about Justin Theroux, he rhapsodizes about the collection of trustworthy behaviors he's exhibited over the years. Think of all the decisions Justin Theroux made to make others feel this way: deciding to pick up the phone, deciding to be loyal and dependable over long periods of time—years, even!

When I think about the types of friendships I want, the way I want my friends to feel about me, this is essentially what I would be thrilled to have them say. If I knew they acknowledged the effort I put in, if they regarded me as a true friend, well, that'd be so freakin' incredible! Let me just beam my good intentions right into their skulls. Unfortunately, that doesn't always happen.

To a soundtrack of clinking coffee cups and humdrum cafe chatter, my friend Katie told me her latest round of IVF didn't take. After spending a small fortune and attending countless doctors' appointments, this procedure—her fifth round of IVF—had failed. Devastated, she didn't have the money or the will to try again. She was never going to be a mother.

I wish I could tell you I hugged her too hard and too long. That I rubbed her back and said, "Yes, today was indeed terrible and unbearably sad." That I assured her I'd be by her side through it all. That I sent her platters of food from the local Italian joint because who could be expected to cook when they were grieving a loss that soul-quaking?

I didn't do any of those things. Instead, seeing my friend consumed with sorrow, my mind went blank. When the silence became overwhelming, I sputtered, "I'm sure it will all work out in the end." She didn't seem buoyed. I panicked: "You'll be a mom one day, Katie. I just know it." I finished my shitty pep talk with a pitiful "You've got this."

As soon as the words left my mouth, I knew I blew the assignment. Discomfort consumed me. Katie's pain was too intense, too raw, too scary. I wanted to fix her sadness, but I had no idea how to do it. Her face fell slack.

Her shoulders slumped. Teary-eyed, she blew her nose, got up, and walked out the door.

This happened in the summer of 2016. I was thirty-eight years old, and I still had no idea how to comfort a grieving friend. I didn't know what to say or how to convey that I cared.

Katie, the friend I saw at the café, ended up ghosting me. My chirpy texts—"Hey girl! Coffee this week?"—went unanswered. To be honest, I get it. I did a crappy job of being there for her. But the fact that yet another one of my friendships had buckled was a throbbing, sensitive wound for me.

I've never been a person who knows the perfect thing to say. I've flubbed it hundreds of times. I thought offering comfort was about stringing the most upbeat words together, almost as if I were trying to convince someone not to feel what they were feeling. *You're sad? Don't be! That thing you're sad about is actually a great thing for you. You're in pain? Just stop. I'm not in pain so you shouldn't be either.*

Now I'm older, and I realize something about offering comfort; I don't have to solve a friend's problem or manage their sorrow. I don't have to crack a secret code to know the perfect things to say. Instead, their pain is a visitor sitting alongside us. The pain is eating a jelly doughnut and blowing on a cup of coffee to cool it down for a sip. It is not my job to usher the visitor away or try to convince my friend that their pain visitor doesn't exist. My job, as a friend, is to acknowledge the visitor sitting with us.

Before I started practicing Wholehearted Friendship, I'd tell a friend in distress, "Don't be sad." I'd probably frown while I was saying it. This strategy wasn't great. All it did was let my friend know that I wasn't going to acknowledge her anguish in any meaningful way.

Now that I know how to be a wholehearted friend, I'll say, "It makes perfect sense why you feel sad (or hurt, frustrated, or disappointed) right now. A painful (hurtful, frustrating, disappointing) thing has happened." I simply validate her experience: *Yes, it's sad that this is happening, and it sucks.*

HOW TO OFFER PRACTICAL HELP

The number one thing people do wrong when offering help is being vague, saying: "Let me know if you need anything." While this sounds like a supportive thing to say, it actually isn't. That's because this phrasing puts the onus on the person suffering to reach out and coordinate help. The majority of people, when they're overwhelmed, grieving, or suffering, will not be enthused about asking others for help.

The best thing you can do when offering help is to specify the help you're willing to offer. Can you walk a dog? Pick up groceries? Mow the lawn? Suggest something your friend can quickly say yes or no to. That's the goal of any suggestions you float.

The key: don't offer to do anything the other person won't reasonably do for you. It can get weird when one friend goes above and beyond for another but that willingness isn't reciprocated. Don't go into debt for a friend who wouldn't cover your movie ticket. You know your friends, so you're in a position to judge what's appropriate. Being mindful of balance lessens resentment.

Here are some ways you can help a struggling friend in times of sadness or loss:

- Make them meal(s)
- Help clean their house or yard
- Send a gift card to a food delivery service
- Sit and listen
- Write a thoughtful card
- Watch their kids or pets
- Put your friend in touch with mental health providers if they're open to it

When offering comfort, assess the situation, pinpoint your friend's concern, then offer to *reasonably* alleviate the concern. I cannot stress this word enough. Yes, it's important for you to be there for your friend, but by no means should you sacrifice your well-being to jump through hundreds of hoops for them or take on their problem as your own. Do what you can with an open and caring heart.

I. **Friend's situation:** She needs to stay late at work due to an emergency.

Friend's chief concern(s): Her dog needs to be walked.

Botched comfort sounds like: "I'm sure your dog will be okay. Don't stress about it."

Actual comfort sounds like: "I can swing by your place and take your pooch for a walk tonight."

Why this comforts your friend: Because it solves her problem, which makes her feel supported.

II. **Friend's situation:** Friend doesn't have enough money to make rent.

Friend's chief concern(s): She'll be evicted if she can't pay rent.

Botched comfort sounds like: "Can you just ask your parents for help paying this month? What about asking your ex? He's rich, right?"

Actual comfort sounds like: "How much money do you need? Let's brainstorm ways you can make some quick cash. In fact, I'll give you $60 to babysit my kiddo for a few hours if you're open to it."

Why this comforts your friend: Because you're thinking of ways to solve her problem of being low on cash. You're showing her you're her teammate who is ready to tackle the problem with her.

III. **Friend's situation:** She's fighting with her significant other. This time it's really bad. She's not sure if she should break up with her partner.

Friend's chief concern(s): A broken heart. She's also not sure where she'll live, as they are cohabitating.

Botched comfort sounds like: "Your partner is a giant asshole anyway. What are you upset about? You can do so much better. Cut the idiot loose. In fact, I'll help you pour bleach on their clothes."

Actual comfort sounds like: "We can get together at the park for iced coffee, and you can tell me what's been going on. Or, I can come to your place with a bottle of wine. You're welcome to crash on my couch for a few days while you clear your head. In the meantime, I'm sending you my therapist's information in case you need someone impartial to listen. Just know that I'm always here for you no matter what."

Why this comforts your friend: Because you're letting her know that you're here for her emotional support, not trying to kick up more drama that could further complicate her life. Obviously, if any abuse is going on, you should help your friend access appropriate support.

IV. **Friend's situation:** She just lost a pet.

Friend's chief concern(s): She had a hard choice to make about putting her beloved pet down, and she's agonizing over it.

Botched comfort sounds like: "It'll be okay. Don't be sad. Think of everything that *is* going right in your life."

Actual comfort sounds like: "You did right by Fluffy. She wasn't in pain at the end. You made the right decision."

Why this comforts your friend: Because it addresses her sorrow at having to make a difficult choice.

Exercise: Offer Comfort

Now you try it.

V. The situation: Friend is moving across the country.

Friend's chief concern(s):

_____

Botched comfort sounds like:

_____

Actual comfort sounds like:

_____

Why this comforts your friend:

_____

VI. The situation: Friend just found out she has a scary medical issue.
Friend's chief concern(s):

_____

Botched comfort sounds like:

_____

Actual comfort sounds like:

_____

Why this comforts your friend:

_____

VII. The situation: Friend is feeling depressed and overwhelmed
    with life.
Friend's chief concern(s):

_____

Botched comfort sounds like:

_____

Actual comfort sounds like:

_____

Why this comforts your friend:

....

You might be tempted to say that you understand your friend's problem because you've gone through a similar experience. This is such a common (entirely preventable!) miscalculation in friendships. Yes, sharing your experience shows empathy on your part. But if you aren't mindful of the *way* you share your experience, it can seem like you're redirecting the conversation to be about you. For example:

Friend #1: (wounded) "I'm so upset. Daniel dumped me."

Friend #2: "Oh, that sucks. I was dumped a few years ago. It absolutely sucked."

Friend #1: "I remember. It was with that guy James, right?"

Friend #2: "Yeah. He dumped me on my birthday, too. Right after I blew out the candles. What an asshole."

Friend #1: (feeling a type of way that we're now focusing on the other person) "Oh, that sucks. On your birthday of all days! That's so heartless."

Friend #2: (bulldozing straight ahead) "Yeah, it was really sad. Heartbreaking, really. I can't even look at cake now without crying. Even crappy snack cakes like Twinkies. Just anything with a cake-like texture. Forget it. Waterworks."

Desired outcome: Friend #2 shared her experience being dumped in hopes that Friend #1 feels supported.

Actual outcome: Friend #1 feels unsupported because Friend #2 made the conversation about herself and her pain.

Likely result: Friend #1 won't want to share details of her relationship with Friend #2 anymore.

Instead, follow up with a few soft questions to subtly direct the conversation back to the friend who's hurting. Let's try this again.

Friend #1: (*wounded*) "Daniel dumped me."

Friend #2: (*concerned*) "Oh, that sucks. I was dumped last year. Right on my birthday too. I can't even look at cake without crying. What did Daniel say? Were you surprised?"

Friend #1: (*sniffling*) "He said we want different things, and he didn't see us getting married. I feel blindsided."

Friend #2: (*frowning*) "Oh, man. That's so painful. I'm heartbroken for you. You really wanted this relationship to go the distance. It's understandable that you're upset. I'm happy to crack his kneecaps if it'll cheer you up. Perhaps break a toe or two. At least a pinkie."

Friend #1: (*smiling*) "No need for violence. At least not yet."

Friend #2: (*comforting*) "Breakups suck. I'll be here for you no matter what. You're not alone. You know that, right? Everyone loves you. We could fill a stadium with your friends! I can even help you create a dating profile when you're ready to get yourself back out there."

Friend #1: (*perking up*) "I'm not there yet, but when I'm ready, I might take you up on that offer."

Desired outcome: Friend #2 shared her own breakup story in order for Friend #1 to feel a sense of camaraderie.

Actual outcome: Friend #1 felt heard and supported because Friend #2 kept the focus on Friend #1 and her breakup. Camaraderie *is* felt.

Likely result: Friend #1 will feel safe being vulnerable with Friend #2.

Let's take another example. This time the issue is work stuff.

Friend #1: (*worried*) "I'm freaking out. I think I might get laid off."

Friend #2: "Oof, that sucks. I was laid off two years ago. It took me eight months to find another job. It was terrible."

Friend #1: (*explaining why she's worried*) "I have no idea what I'll do if I lose this gig. I really need the money."

Friend #2: (*minimizing the friend's concerns*) "Oh, you'll find something soon. The new job will be better for you, probably. I mean, look at me now! I love working at my job. I'm actually low-key grateful I got laid off because I never would've found this position otherwise. It's like I always say, 'Everything happens for a reason.'"

Desired outcome: Friend #1 feels buoyed because Friend #2 shared how she bounced back from a setback at work.

Actual outcome: Friend #1 feels like Friend #2 dismissed her sensible worries.

Likely result: Friend #1 won't want to share hardships with Friend #2 anymore.

Let's tweak this conversation. Take two!

Friend #1: (*worried*) "I'm freaking out. I think I might get laid off."

Friend #2: (*sympathizing*) "Oh, that sucks. I was laid off two years ago. It took me eight months to find another job. It was a really scary time. What have you done so far to prepare? Have you put some feelers out to see if there are any openings for anything else in your field?"

Friend #1: (*focused*) "I updated my LinkedIn profile. I was thinking about reaching out to some of our competitors to see if any of them are hiring."

Friend #2: (*pumping her up*) "That's a great idea! You know, my brother-in-law Eric works for one of those competitors. I can reach out to him and see if there are any opportunities at his company."

Friend #1: (*hopeful*) "I would love that."

Friend #2: (*reassuring*) "Absolutely. Layoffs are tough. It's great that you have a sterling reputation and robust network. I'm happy to take a look at your résumé and help you spruce it up if you want. Get you in fighting shape."

Friend #1: (*smiling, relieved*) "That would be great! I will definitely take you up on that."

Desired outcome: Friend #1 feels hopeful because Friend #2 shared how she bounced back from a setback at work and put her network to use.

Actual outcome: Friend #1 feels like Friend #2 is empathetic to her situation and feels supported knowing that Friend #2 will help her navigate whatever comes her way.

Likely result: Friend #1 will be sure to keep Friend #2 in the loop as the job situation develops.

What's remarkable about these techniques is that they're so simple yet so effective. Once we realize what help and comfort look and sound like, it's easier to offer it instinctively.

Regardless of what you say, sometimes people are going to be in a crummy mood and will snap at you. You might say everything in a perfect, nonthreatening way and you still might feel like you didn't nail the brief. When people are in emotional, mental, or physical pain, they might have trouble regulating their tone or expressing appreciation. Resist the urge to take this personally.

HOW TO BE CURIOUS

Being interested in other people may not come naturally to you. It certainly hasn't for me. My family isn't great at asking each other questions. If anything, asking too many questions is seen as prying or invasive. Growing up, it was assumed if you had something to share, then you'd pipe up at the dinner table. Conversely, my husband's parents peppered him with questions when he was a kid. It was how they showed they cared and took interest in him and his life. Mike and I have had several conversations about the importance of asking each other questions because we have very different ideas about what asking questions means: I'm afraid to pry and put him on the spot. He's looking to see if I'm even interested in his life.

Most friends expect that you'll take an interest in their inner life. For people like me, that's intimidating. I sometimes look at someone and just draw a blank when it comes to asking them questions, which is hilarious because I'm a working journalist. Of course when I'm naturally curious, questions flow out of me. But when I'm indifferent or uncertain, I clam up. Maybe you're afraid of being intrusive or saying the wrong thing when asking others questions. That's understandable.

But it's worth learning how to be curious about other people in a way that lets them open up to you. In her book *We Should Get Together: The Secret to Cultivating Better Friendship*, connection expert Kat Vellos offers a robust selection of questions to invite conversation with your friends with a range of things like reflection, imagination, identity, relationships, learning, and society.[2]

- What's a memory you really love?
- What have you been thinking about a lot lately?
- If you were to become famous for something in the next year, what would you want to be famous for?
- What's something you think would be fun to try doing?
- In what ways are you weird?
- What's something you think about that other people seem to never think about?
- What's something valuable you learned from an ex?

Asking thoughtful questions like these helps expand your friendship and allows you to get to know your friend for the multidimensional person they are. Vellos has created conversation calendars and cards to help all of us who struggle to move the conversation along.

In her book *The Fine Art of Small Talk*, Debra Fine recommends opening a conversation with basically anyone by asking, "What keeps you busy?"[3] This phrasing allows the conversation to flow in countless directions. "It's an excellent query that does not pigeonhole others based on what they do for a living, if they are married, or if they have children," she wrote.

She even suggests tailoring the question to the situation you're in:

- "What keeps you busy outside of work?"
- "What keeps you busy outside of eating Sweetgreen salads?"
- "What keeps you busy outside of school?"
- "What keeps you busy outside of cleaning teeth?" This one is really only effective for dental hygienists.

Fine's also a fan of the statement + question conversation starter. This way it's clear you're initiating a conversation, not just mumbling to yourself.

Instead of: "Wow, what a movie."

Try: "Wow, what a movie. What did you think of the lead performance?"

Instead of: "I love your necklace!"

Try: "I love your necklace. Where did you get it?"

Instead of: "I'm a fan of that new café down the street."

Try: "I'm a fan of that new café down the street. Where do you like to grab a cup of coffee?"

These structural changes to your conversations are easy to incorporate and make a world of difference when trying to nurture connection. It's not just what you say to a friend that matters, but the actions and intent behind it. To ensure your friends feel safe and cared for in your presence, it's important that you engage with them in a way that acknowledges both the good and bad. It's the ups and downs of life that make us who we are, so it's important that we embrace both.

18

Taming Your Inner Yoda

One of my closest friends asked me if she should kick her boyfriend to the curb. Between us, she should've dumped him eons ago. I hesitated sharing that with her because I didn't think she'd ultimately take my (wise, reasonable, caring) advice.

It's understandable why I debated telling her my opinion: people love tossing in their two cents when they see someone struggling. In fact, giving advice increases one's sense of personal power. That's because it gives the adviser a perceived influence over others' actions, according to a study published in the *Personality and Social Psychology Bulletin*.[1]

Another issue the study uncovered: people with a high tendency to seek power are more likely to give advice than those with a low tendency to seek power. If you're a power seeker, giving others advice might feel irresistible.

You know how we all crave feeling like we matter? What's more fulfilling than hearing a person you value say: *I took your advice and my life is better for it*. It's basically emotional catnip.

The problem is that advice isn't given in a vacuum. There are all sorts of power dynamics flying around when one person assumes the role of adviser in a relationship of equals, such as a peer friendship.

Another hitch to dispensing advice like Pez candy: giving thoughtless or unsolicited advice will hinder the closeness you crave. Offering advice without considering the nuances of a situation can alienate the person you are giving advice to. That's because you're essentially telling them you know their life better than they do. That comes off as arrogant and insensitive.

It's easy for me to suggest that a friend dump their partner because I don't have to experience the consequences of the decision. I don't have to find a new way to meet several of my basic needs:

- Survival, if the couple lives together and/or shares finances
- Power, if they enjoy a certain social status
- Love and belonging, which the romantic relationship could provide
- Freedom, if the relationship was a large part of their identity
- Fun, if they had pleasurable rituals or inside jokes

Not every relationship provides those needs, but many do. Obviously, again, if any abuse is going on, it's essential to offer your support and gently point your friend towards the appropriate resources.

We've all had that friend who can't resist chiming in with everything we should or shouldn't do to navigate an issue.

Friend: My mother-in-law is driving me up the wall.
Wannabe Yoda: You should block her on your phone.

Friend: I haven't had a vacation in three years.
Wannabe Yoda: You should go to Iceland.

Friend: I can't stand my boss.
Wannabe Yoda: You should quit your job.

These are all of the ways that a Wannabe Yoda attempts to control what their friend should do or think. Hey, I'm a recovering Wannabe Yoda. I know how seductive giving advice can be.

People want to help others, sure. They also want to help others in a way that boosts their own self-esteem. We love to think of ourselves as a Yoda just wandering the land blessing people with our pearls of wisdom. Your spouse hasn't been affectionate lately? Dump him, you must. Watching the news depresses you? Get off social media and disable notifications, young Jedi. (That's actually good advice. See? Sometimes a Wannabe Yoda's advice is not horrible. Which is why we keep bringing up our problems to them.)

But just because you're comfortable giving others guidance doesn't necessarily mean people will take it. In fact, researchers identified three factors that determine whether advice will be taken:[2]

1. **People will take advice if it was costly to attain or if a task is difficult.** If you can't make heads or tails of a contract, you're more likely to follow your lawyer's advice. Especially if they charge $500/hour. And if you're looking to rip out a wall in your kitchen to install an island (I'm jealous because it's my dream to have a kitchen island), you're more likely to go along with a contractor's suggestions.

2. **People will take advice if the person offering counsel is more experienced and expresses extreme confidence in the quality of their counsel.** When my doctor told me my cholesterol was high, I cut down on dairy and butter because she knows what she's talking about. When my favorite beauty influencer hailed the new Kosas Revealer Concealer as the best concealer she's ever used, I purchased a tube because she's tested every product on the market.

3. **People will disregard advice when strong emotion plays a role.** Decision makers are more likely to disregard advice if they feel certain about what's best or if they're angry. When passions run high, your influence might be limited no matter how calmly you make your case. For instance, when fuming, a friend might send a rage text to their ex if they're dead set on it even though you explain how that's ill advised.

Understanding when people are likely to take—or disregard—advice will help you make wiser decisions when offering counsel because you'll know when you're more likely to move the needle. Oftentimes we give advice to our friends with the best of intentions. Generally speaking, we really do want what's best for them in their personal and professional lives.

HOW TO GIVE ADVICE WITHOUT ALIENATING OTHERS

Giving advice is tricky because the act of telling someone what they should do is laden with power dynamics.

Before you give advice:

1. Determine if you're qualified to give advice.

2. Ask what actions they've already taken.

3. Offer an out by saying, "Feel free to ignore anything I say that's unhelpful." It releases the other person from believing they have to engage with your counsel.

While you give your advice:

1. Resist using the word *should*. It can feel domineering if used thoughtlessly. Instead of saying, "You should break up with him," soften the advice with, "If it were me, I'd strongly consider if this was a relationship I'd want to stay in."

2. Watch your friend's body language. See if they seem receptive to your advice or not. Do they maintain eye contact? Are they nodding along? Taking notes? All good signs.

3. Give one or two ideas and ask for feedback. "How am I doing? Are you finding any of these things helpful? Would you like more suggestions?"

After you give your advice:

1. Ask if they'd be interested in you sending them additional resources like a relevant book, online course, or podcast.

2. Ask if any follow-up is needed. Do they want you to check in on them? Do they want to meet again to talk about the issue? Ask!

Exercise

Let's try giving advice to a friend in a wholehearted way.

I. Friend: "I think my child might have a learning disability."

_____

II. Friend: "I'm not getting along with my in-laws."

_____

III. Friend: "I'm thinking about quitting my job."

_____

IV. Friend: "I heard from my ex. He said he wants to get back together."

_____

RESIST PROBLEM-SOLVING

When you resist the tempting urge to affix a Band-Aid to the problem, peace is more likely to occur. Oftentimes with friends, they don't want us—nor do they expect us—to solve their problems. Usually, they just want a sympathetic ear. The next time a friend vents to you, just validate what they tell you:

- "Yes, that does sound hard."
- "It makes perfect sense you'd feel that way."
- "I'm gutted for you. You deserved better."
- "I'm frustrated on your behalf."

When it comes to friendships, problem-solving is one of the areas where you can absolutely do less. Hang back, validate your friend's feelings, and just be present. That's the secret because that's what our friends *really* want us to do. So work on doing just that.

MOVING FORWARD

Hooray! We've covered how to be a respectful, caring friend who approaches their friends like a true teammate. You now know that wholehearted friendships need desire, diligence, and delight, and you're equipped with the knowledge and skills to not only build healthy friendships but maintain the wonderful ones you currently have. I hope you now feel empowered to go out in the world and be the best friend you can be both to yourself and others.

Did you have any light bulb moments while reading the book? Did you gain clarity on any aspects of your cherished friendships? Follow me on social media at @AnnaGoldfarb and share your friendship successes and insights.

14-Day Friendship Cleanse

If, after reading this book, you're thinking, *Anna, just tell me what to do to make some big changes quickly,* here are two weeks of tips, activities, and advice that will help you wholeheartedly connect with new pals, old pals, and everyone in between.

DAY 1: START FRESH

Today we are wiping the slate clean. All those times you didn't know the perfect thing to say, how to express that you cared, or how to offer support? Forgive yourself! For real, you did the best you could with the information you had. Today is a new day. Our goal with this friendship cleanse is to make a few strategic adjustments to how you approach others. No big moves. Just small, smart steps.

Today's mission: Toss out at least three things that no longer serve you—a lipstick you never liked, a dusty DVD on your shelf you'll never watch, a T-shirt that never fit right. Just chuck it. Or give it away. Don't overthink it. Clear out the clutter. We're starting this two-week friendship cleanse on a happy, hopeful note. There's no bitterness. No remorse. No judgment, even. Just as some thoughts and behaviors in your past relationships no longer work for you, these items don't work for you either, so they can go.

DAY 2: ACCOUNTING

Identify who is in your current inner circle. If you're in transition or have just moved to a new place, you may not have a lot of names to jot down.

That's okay. Just consider who would be in those tiers for you. It will likely change as you find your social footing. Make a list of:

- One to two people in your **bathtub**. This is your most intimate tier. It's usually a significant other and/or a best friend.

- Three to five people in your **Jacuzzi**. These are your closest friends, your support tier.

- Ten to fifteen people in your **swimming pool**. This could be work friends, school friends, relatives, other couples you go on double dates with, and so on.

This list is your intimate social network. These are the people whose friendship matters the most to you. These are your peeps, as someone from the aughts would say; the people you seek out, spend time with, encourage, and support.

DAY 3: COMMITMENT

Commit to showing up for the short list of people you indicated were in your bathtub, Jacuzzi, and swimming pool tiers. This is your inner circle, your ride-or-dies. Make sure you have all their birthdays written in your calendar. If they have children, note their children's birthdays in your calendar too. Also make sure you have their mailing addresses and updated contact info.

Remember, the bathtub and Jacuzzi tiers encompass the people for whom you will:

- Get together with them at every opportunity

- Be in frequent contact with them

- Make every effort to attend their milestone events

- Remember their birthday. (Give them a gift or make some appropriate gesture.)

- Have a small budget for holiday gifts for them and their family
- Vow to answer their calls and texts ASAP

For the swimming pool tier, you will expect to:

- Be reasonably close and stay in loose contact with them
- Make some effort to attend their milestone events
- Remember their birthday (Gifts are optional, depending on your relationship.)
- Answer their calls and texts within a day or two

DAY 4: GOAL SETTING

You won't know if you're successful unless you define what success in friendships mean to you. For one person, friendship success could look like having a monthly coffee date with a buddy. For another person, success could look like giving great gifts from now on, especially if gifting doesn't come easy to you.

Write down your one-year friendship goals. Brainstorm things you would like to do with your close friends. Sometimes goals can also look like behaviors you'd like to avoid, like ghosting, flaking, or bailing. Maybe your goal is to stop interrupting your friends or learn how to offer comfort. Be specific. Your list could look like:

- Be part of a group that meets together regularly
- Throw myself a small birthday party
- Take a vacation with a friend
- Get to know my neighbors
- Embrace saying no to people

Just by identifying a goal, you're taking the first step to modifying your behavior and making these accomplishments more likely to happen.

DAY 5: DILIGENCE

Set reminders in your phone or calendar to check in with the friends you'd love to be closer to. Maybe it's once every two weeks. Maybe it's monthly. Whatever feels right for you. Take notes during your conversations about anything important that pops up, like upcoming doctors' appointments, vacations, or big career happenings. Recently, a friend in my Jacuzzi tier competed in a triathlon so I made sure to text her good luck before the event. Afterwards, I asked how it went.

Also, pay attention to any bids your friends make, as well as significant events coming up for them, like work milestones, birthdays, or an anniversary of a loved one's passing. Being on top of these noteworthy dates will let your friends know you care about them, and that you recognize them for all the roles they play in their life.

DAY 6: DESIRE

Reach out to one acquaintance you'd like to get to know better. Give a clear and compelling reason to meet in the next two week or so. Say something like, "Hey! You've been on my mind. Any interest in joining me for X in order to Y?" That could be:

- To eat ramen so I can hear about your new job

- To get a manicure and talk about the trips you have coming up this summer

- To join me for a lecture at the museum that looks interesting

- To meet in the park and share what books, TV shows, and podcasts we've been loving

DAY 7: AUTOMATION

Automate your interactions to take the guesswork out of planning a meetup. Set a recurring date with one friend. It can be a monthly phone date. Or a weekly co-working session. The key is that the activity (1) is clear and compelling for both people, and (2) requires scant communication to keep the date:

- "Are we still on for our jog on Friday morning?" "Yup!"

- "Are we still on for our Thursday yoga class?"
  "Looking forward to it!"

- "I might be a little late to book club, but I'll be there."
  "I'll be there too."

DAY 8: DELIGHT

Text positive messages to up to three friends. Tell them how much their friendship means to you. Say something like, "I just want you to know that I love you so much. I'm grateful for our friendship. There's no need to write back if you're busy. Feel free to tap back with a heart. It's all good!"

Extra credit: Offer them a genuine compliment. List three reasons why you love being their friend. Are they intelligent, hilarious, thoughtful, caring, or brave? Tell them!

DAY 9: VULNERABILITY

See if there's a friend in your Jacuzzi or swimming pool that might be out of the loop with you. Set a date to share what's really going on in your lives. Be vulnerable. "Want to grab lunch on Sunday and fill me in on what's been going on with you? I'm thinking about how you've been stretched thin and juggling everything. That can't be easy."

DAY 10: TAKING BIDS

Solicit your friends for ideas about what to watch or listen to next. You can even prompt them with what you're in the mood for: a comedy, documentary, true crime podcast, etc. Then, engage with whatever shows or movies your friends suggest. Reach out to them and let them know your thoughts about what they recommended. It makes people feel good when their advice is taken. Give your friends the gift of feeling like their suggestions matter to you.

DAY 11: FAVORS

Ask a friend for a low-stakes favor. It can be asking them to teach you something or take you somewhere. This can sound like, "I love how you're always going on morning hikes. Will you show me some of your favorite trails?" Or "I know you're been practicing learning how to read tarot cards. Can you do a tarot reading for me if I buy you lunch?"

By initiating an act of service, you might develop a new appreciation for your friend. You'll also learn more about what they're passionate about. This could even expand the focus of your friendship.

DAY 12: REKINDLE

Send a low-stakes message to a friend you've lost touch with, possibly someone who moved from your Jacuzzi to your swimming pool. Make it breezy and keep expectations low. Say something like, "Hey! You've been on my mind. Remember that time we did [something silly or wild]? I still crack up about it! I hope you're well." Your friend may no longer be at the Jacuzzi level, but you're learning to appreciate the friendship for what it is today. Look at us being mature! *high-five*

If you're looking for further connection with this person, you can certainly float that idea: "If you ever want to get together more regularly, I'm open to it. Are you still obsessed with skin care? We could get facials. Or, maybe we could join a gym together and take classes. Could be fun."

DAY 13: MINDFULLY VENT

It's easy to take our friends' willingness to listen for granted. While it feels good to unload, it's not always pleasurable to be the recipient of someone's unloading. No one wants to be bitched at, especially if they have their own issues they're dealing with. It's rude to take advantage of people like that. Be mindful of how your venting impacts your friends.

Today, ask for consent before you vent to a close friend. Be explicit about what you need in the moment: "I'm just looking to vent about my boss for a few minutes. No advice needed. You game?" Or, "Is it a good time for me to complain about a client? It's not urgent, but if you have five minutes to lend an ear today, let me know."

Reducing uncertainty is a wonderful gift to give your friends. By being up front with your needs: (Please listen, don't pepper me with advice), you're setting you both up for success.

DAY 14: MAKE MEANING

For the last day of the cleanse, think about starting a ritual with each of your Jacuzzi friends to honor your individual relationship. This can look like:

- Celebrating a friendiversary by going out to your favorite restaurant
- Throwing a Friendsgiving party together this year
- Attending a concert of your favorite band
- Exchanging matching bracelets or rings
- Having a yearly "watch our favorite John Hughes movie" party
- Going to a karaoke bar and performing a duet

Do what feels right for you both. When you make space to celebrate your magical connection, you send the message that you—and your bond—matters. What a glorious feeling!

In the future, if you lose your way, reread the chapters that walk you through the common reasons friendships cool off. We're living in a world that makes it incredibly difficult to sustain lifelong friendships. This doesn't mean we should give up; it just means we have to work a little harder—and smarter—to enjoy our wonderful modern friendships.

Acknowledgments

Writing a book about our friendships has been a deeply personal and rewarding experience. First and foremost, I want to express my deepest thanks to my wonderful family. Their love and encouragement have meant the world to me. My sister Sarah Schwartz has been an excellent cheerleader at every step of the way. My brother-in-law Alex Rolfe has helped immensely with revisions and useful comments. (He always has the best wine to share too.) My sister Rachel Rolfe is a testament to the power of how life-changing the power of the Wholehearted Friendship paradigm can be. To be best friends with my sister? How lucky can I get??? She has spent countless hours talking through these concepts with me. She also helped articulate my vision for the cover design. She's my collaborator, no question about it.

To the kiddos—Julianna Schwartz, Henry Rolfe, Tilly Rolfe, and Eloise Rolfe—they are my collective sunshine. My mission is to (hopefully) make their world a better, more friendship-friendly place. My mother, Arlene Goldfarb, is my #1 fan. I'm awed by her strength and resilience, as she's rebuilt her life after so much pain. Thank you for believing in me, Mom. I know my dad, Roy Goldfarb, would be thrilled that his life was an inspiration for this project. Being his daughter made me want to make him proud. His passing made me want to start a larger conversation about what modern friendship means to all of us. I miss him—and his belly laughs—eternally. My husband, Mike, has been a perfect partner throughout this process. Sometimes I feel like he must've been custom created for me, like I went down to the Build-A-Husband store at the Cherry Hill Mall and had him stitched together to my exact specifications. He's the love of my life, and creating our little family with Eleanor is my greatest joy and proudest accomplishment.

To my friends, who have been a constant source of inspiration and motivation, thank you for showing me how special friendships can be. Alexis Rosenzweig has not only shown me what a loving friendship looks like, but in writing this book, I've learned she's ridiculously fun to travel with too! I've learned that when I listen to her advice, my life gets unequivocally better. Thank you, Alexis, for your help negotiating contracts and providing valuable insights. You're so generous, intelligent, and caring. I love you. Thank you, Reed Barrow, Hudson Barrow, Penelope Barrow, and Pippi Barrow for being part of my chosen family. Thank you, Jenna Davis, for our treasured decades-long friendship. No one on this planet makes me laugh as hard as you do! If I'm ever in a funk, I know you're one Diamond Dave gif away from a legit mood booster. Thank you, Tracy Wilson, for being a sister to me. Tracy was my first friendship role model. She surrounds herself with interesting people and she makes them feel valued by being kind, warm, and patient. I cannot overstate how much you've influenced me, Tracy. I'm forever grateful to you for the many lessons you've taught me about how to make people feel loved and seen.

Writing is a team sport, and I'm lucky to have the best teammates around. Thank you, Allie Volpe, for being an incredible source of camaraderie and love. I can say with certainty that together we can accomplish anything! Having you in my corner has changed my life and pushed me further than I could've gone on my own. Your friendship is truly the key to my success. Tim Herrera is the best editor I've ever worked with. Working with him on dozens of stories for the *New York Times* has been the highlight of my career. His interest and support have changed my life in countless ways for the better.

I extend my sincere appreciation to my brilliant agent, Sonali Chanchani, whose guidance and wise expertise have been instrumental in shaping these ideas and refining my writing. Her invaluable notes and thoughtful suggestions have made this book richer and one thousand times more compelling.

Thank you to the talented professionals who brought this book to life. From the jump, my editor, Diana Ventimiglia, connected with my vision for this book. She immediately understood the need for a book like this, which was incredibly validating. She's also been an absolute joy to work with. Thank you, Diana, for your unwavering support and enthusiasm. Lyric Dodson's notes and comments have improved the manuscript beyond measure. The design team skillfully translated the essence of my book into a vibrant and evocative cover. To the entire publishing team at Sounds True, thank you for your hard work and dedication to making this dream of a book into the reality you hold in your hands (or read on your device).

My gratitude also extends to the individuals who generously shared their (sometimes painful) experiences with me. Their stories have enriched the book. Thank you to the experts, academics, and psychologists who shared their wisdom.

I'm deeply thankful to my readers for going on this journey with me. Their engagement with my work has been a constant boost.

I'm grateful for the many connections I've have made through this experience: my book buddy Ellen Hendriksen has been a perfect companion. Thank you, Ellen, for your wisdom and compassion. My weekly book chats with Cece Xie and Melissa Petro kept me on track and gave me lots of food for thought. Nina Badzin, thank you for bringing these friendship issues to the forefront in your podcast. If we lived closer to one another, we'd definitely be pals.

My cohorts—Marisa G. Franco, Danielle Bayard Jackson, Adam "Smiley" Poswolsky, Shasta Nelson, Natalie Lue, Kat Vellos, and Miriam Kirmayer—it's an honor to have you all as colleagues in this friendship space. These are all excellent resources on friendships, people. Seek their content out and thank me later!

Juli Fraga has been a warm presence in this project. Our friendship spans time zones! Hearing about her cat Oreo's mishaps has been a constant source of merriment in my household.

My movie matinee and Dan Dan noodles buddy, Jen A. Miller, has been a reliable source of support as well. An incredible writer, her notes helped me shape the section where I talked about my dad's passing. I'm so grateful to you for helping me with that, Jen. Also her (many!) postcards from the road made me smile.

Thank you to my fellow Philly creatives who inspire me: R. Eric Thomas, Eric Smith, Tara Jacoby, Adam Teterus, and Gina Tomaine. Thank you to my double-date buddies, Chip Chantry and Kim Chantry. Mike and I promise to always split a Caesar salad with you both until the end of time.

Lastly, thank you to the countless unnamed individuals whose contributions, in big and small ways, have played a part in shaping this book. From the semi-strangers at local cafes who shared their own stories with me to the serendipitous encounter at a small house party in Laurel Canyon that sparked new ideas, thank you for being a part of this journey.

To everyone mentioned here and to those whose names might not appear but have had a positive impact on my life, I am indebted to each one of you. This book would not be what it is without your involvement. On a personal note, I wouldn't be here without the power of these friendships. They've all changed my life for the better. I hope, with the help of this book, everyone gets to experience the heights of true wholehearted friendship.

Notes

INTRODUCTION

1 Daniel A. Cox, "The State of American Friendship: Change, Challenges, and Loss," The Survey Center on American Life, June 8, 2021, americansurveycenter.org/research/the-state-of-american -friendship-change-challenges-and-loss/.

2 Kumal Bhattacharya et al., "Sex differences in social focus across the life cycle in humans," *Royal Society Open Science*, vols. 3, 4 (April 6, 2016): 160097, doi:10.1098/rsos.160097.

3 NWO (Netherlands Organization for Scientific Research), "Half of Your Friends Lost in Seven Years, Social Network Study Finds," ScienceDaily, May 27, 2009, sciencedaily.com/releases/2009/05/090527111907.htm.

CHAPTER 1: MODERN FRIENDSHIP IS WILD

1 Cezary Jan Strusiewicz, "Medals of Friendship: The Heartwarming Story of the 1936 Olympics," *Tokyo Weekender*, July 20, 2021.

2 William Deresiewicz, "Faux Friendship," Chronicle.com, December 6, 2020, chronicle.com/article/faux-friendship/.

3 Anna Sánchez-Juárez, "Why Is It Harder to Make Friends after 30?" Universitat Oberta de Catalunya, February 2, 2018.

4 Julianne Holt-Lunstad, Timothy B. Smith, and J. Bradley Layton, "Social Relationships and Mortality Risk: A Meta-Analytic Review," *PLoS Medicine* 7, no. 7 (July 27, 2010).

5 Daniel A. Cox, "The State of American Friendship: Change, Challenges, and Loss," The Survey Center on American Life, June 8, 2021.

6 "Public Trust in Government: 1958-2022," Pew Research Center, U.S. Politics & Policy, June 6, 2022.

7 Lee Rainie, Scott Keeter, and Andrew Perrin, "Americans' Trust in Government, Each Other, Leaders," Pew Research Center, U.S. Politics & Policy, July 22, 2019.

8 Menelaos Apostolou et al., "Why friendships end: An evolutionary examination," *Evolutionary Behavioral Sciences* 16, no. 4 (2022): 30–42.

9 Jeffrey A. Hall, "How Many Hours Does It Take to Make a Friend?" *Journal of Social and Personal Relationships* 36, no. 4 (March 15, 2018): 1278–96.

10 Menelaos Apostolou and Despoina Keramari, "What Prevents People from Making Friends: A Taxonomy of Reasons," *Personality and Individual Differences* 163 (September 1, 2020): 110043.

11 Apostolou and Keramari.

12 Sarah Epstein, "5 Reasons People Stay in Unhappy Friendships," *Psychology Today*, July 6, 2021.

CHAPTER 2: SIX HARD TRUTHS
ABOUT MODERN FRIENDSHIP

1 Don Miguel Ruiz, *The Four Agreements* (Carlsbad, CA: Hay House, Inc., 2008), 48–50.

2 John Gottman and Joan Declaire, *The Relationship Cure: A Five-Step Guide to Strengthening Your Marriage, Family, and Friendships* (New York: Three Rivers Press, 2002), 4–18.

3 Suzanne Degges-White and Marcela Kepic, "Friendships, Subjective Age, and Life Satisfaction of Women in Midlife," *Adultspan Journal* 19, no. 1 (April 2020): 39–53.

4 James K. Rilling et al., "A Neural Basis for Social Cooperation," *Neuron* 35, no. 2 (July 2002): 395–405.

5 Degges-White and Kepic, "Friendships, Subjective Age, and Life Satisfaction of Women in Midlife."

CHAPTER 3: WHY YOU FEEL LIKE YOU HAVE BOTH 100 FRIENDS AND ZERO FRIENDS

1   Georg Simmel, translated by Kurt W. Wolff and Reinhard Bendix, "Conflict and the Web of Group-Affiliations," (Glencoe, Illinois: The Free Press, 1955), 195; *American Political Science Review* 49, no. 4 (December 1955): 1213.

2   Bernice A. Pescosolido and Beth A. Rubin, "The Web of Group Affiliations Revisited: Social Life, Postmodernism, and Sociology," *American Sociological Review* 65, no. 1 (February 2000): 52–76.

3   Pescosolido and Rubin, 62–63.

4   Pescosolido and Rubin, 64.

5   Pescosolido and Rubin, 64.

6   Pescosolido and Rubin, 64.

7   Daniel Cox, "The State of American Friendship: Change, Challenges, and Loss," The Survey Center on American Life, June 8, 2021.

8   Janice McCabe, "Friends with Academic Benefits," *Contexts* 15, no. 3 (August 2016): 22–29.

9   McCabe.

10 McCabe.

11 Jeffrey A. Hall, interview by author, Philadelphia, February 14, 2023.

CHAPTER 4: WHY WE CRAVE FRIENDSHIPS EVEN THOUGH PEOPLE ARE BAFFLING

1   William Glasser, *Choice Theory: A New Psychology of Personal Freedom* (New York: Harper Perennial, 1998), 71.

2   Glasser, 25–43.

3   Menelaos Apostolou et al., "Why People Make Friends: The Nature of Friendship," *Personal Relationships* 28, no. 1 (November 18, 2020).

4   Kumal Bhattacharya et al. "Sex differences in social focus across the life cycle in humans," *Royal Society Open Science*, vols. 3, 4 (April 6, 2016): 160097, doi:10.1098/rsos.160097.

5   Daniel A. Cox, "The State of American Friendship: Change, Challenges, and Loss," The Survey Center on American Life, June 8, 2021.

6   Shasta Nelson, interview by author, Philadelphia, May 18, 2017.

7 Geoffrey L. Grief, interview by author, May 17, 2017.

8 Grief.

9 Shasta Nelson, interview by author, Philadelphia, May 18, 2017.

10 Nelson.

11 Eugene Kennedy, *On Being a Friend* (Ballantine Books, 1987), 109.

12 "Clarity Is the Most Important Thing. I Can Compare Clarity . . ." QuoteTab, accessed August 20, 2023, quotetab.com/quote/by-diane -von-furstenberg/clarity-is-the-most-important-thing-i-can -compare-clarity-to-pruning-in-gardenin ?source=vision.

CHAPTER 5: BATHTUBS, JACUZZIS, AND SWIMMING POOLS, OH MY!

1 Robin Dunbar, *Friends* (Little, Brown Book Group, 2021), 69–72.

CHAPTER 6: WHY WE HAVE THE FRIENDS WE DO

1 Daniel A. Cox, "The State of American Friendship: Change, Challenges, and Loss," The Survey Center on American Life, June 8, 2021.

2 Suzanne Degges-White, "Friendology: The Science of Friendship," *Psychology Today*, 2018.

3 Carolyn Weisz, interview by author, Philadelphia, February 14, 2023.

CHAPTER 7: CAN WE TRUST OUR INTUITION WHEN PICKING FRIENDS?

1 "Intuition," *Psychology Today*, psychologytoday.com/ us/basics /intuition.

2 Galang Lufityanto, Chris Donkin, and Joel Pearson, "Measuring Intuition," *Psychological Science* 27, no. 5 (April 6, 2016): 622–34.

3 Daniel Kahneman, "Maps of Bounded Rationality: A Perpective on Intuitive Judgement and Choice," 2002, nobelprize.org /uploads/2018/06/kahnemann-lecture.pdf.

4 Socrates, Quotes.net, retrieved July 27, 2023, quotes.net/quote/932.

5   Eugene Kennedy, "Catholicism's Central Teaching: How to Be
    Imperfect," *National Catholic Reporter*, October 19, 2012,
    ncronline.org/blogs/bulletins-human-side
    /catholicisms-central-teaching-how-be-imperfect.

CHAPTER 8: HAPPY PEOPLE DO THIS
ONE THING INSTINCTIVELY

1   Tom Rath, *Vital Friends: The People You Can't Afford to Live Without*
    (Gallup Press, 2006), 35–38.
2   Rath, 37.
3   "What Are Workplace Buddies Worth?" Gallup, October 12, 2006,
    news.gallup.com/businessjournal/24883/ what-workplace-buddies
    -worth.aspx.

CHAPTER 9: WHY FRIENDSHIPS FAIL

1   "Deadly and Connecting Habits," William Glasser Institute, accessed
    August 19, 2023, glassermsr.com/deadly-and-connecting-habits/.
2   John Gottman and Joan Declaire, *The Relationship Cure: A Five-Step
    Guide to Strengthening Your Marriage, Family, and Friendships* (New
    York: Three Rivers Press, 2002), 264–74.
3   "Deadly and Connecting Habits."
4   Sarah Epstein, "5 Reasons People Stay in Unhappy Friendships,"
    Psychology Today, July 6, 2021, psychologytoday.com/ us/blog
    /between-the-generations/202107/5-reasons-people-stay-in-unhappy
    -friendships.
5   Heather Havrilesky, "Ask Polly: 'Should I Dump My Toxic Friend?'"
    The Cut, May 2, 2018.

CHAPTER 10: DESIRE, DILIGENCE, AND DELIGHT

1   Marisa Franco, interview by author, Philadelphia, May 6, 2023.

CHAPTER 11: THE SECRET TO GETTING A HELL YES! EVERY TIME

1 Adam Teterus, interview by author, Philadelphia, April 10, 2023.

2 Octavius A. Newman and Adam Teterus, *Comic Book Junto: #042: I Have Mutagens In My Blood*, October 6, 2016, open.spotify.com/episode/0aRiZ76fQ3YHnEkAZZNaXP.

3 Adam Teterus, interview by author, Philadelphia, April 10, 2023.

4 Robin Dunbar, *Friends* (Little, Brown Book Group, 2021), 200–206.

5 C. S. Lewis, *The Four Loves* (San Francisco: Harvest Books, 1971), 66–67.

6 Lewis, 66.

7 Dunbar, *Friends*, 203.

8 Gail Matthews, "The Impact of Commitment, Accountability, and Written Goals on Goal Achievement," Psychology Faculty Presentations, January 1, 2007, scholar.dominican.edu /psychology-faculty-conference-presentations/3.

CHAPTER 12: INITIATORS, RISE UP!

1 Christian Langkamp, *Practical Friendship* (Books on Demand, 2021).

2 Suzanne Degges-White, interview by author, Philadelphia, April 17, 2023.

3 Meik Wiking, *The Art of Making Memories: How to Create and Remember Happy Moments* (New York: William Morrow, 2019), 14–15.

4 Meik Wiking, interview by author, Philadelphia, March 22, 2023.

5 Katherine Handcock, "Pilots in Evening Gowns: When Amelia Earhart and Eleanor Roosevelt Took to the Skies," April 20, 2023, amightygirl.com/blog?p=25357.

6 Jeffrey A. Hall et al., "Quality Conversation Can Increase Daily Well-Being," *Communication Research*, January 27, 2023.

7 Danielle Bayard Jackson, interview by author, Philadelphia, February 27, 2023.

8 Ellen Hendriksen, interview by author, Philadelphia, February, 8, 2023.

CHAPTER 13: THE UNBEATABLE POWER OF A FLEXIBLE MINDSET

1 Jenée Desmond-Harris, "Help! My Niece's Elopement Plan Is about to Tear Our Family Apart," *Slate*, August 18, 2022.

2 Suzanne Degges-White and Judy Pochel Van Tieghem, *Toxic Friendships: Knowing the Rules and Dealing with the Friends Who Break Them* (Lanham: Rowman & Littlefield, 2015), 74.

3 Kiaundra Jackson, interview by author, Philadelphia, October 5, 2022.

4 Jackson.

5 Parks Australia, "History of Uluru-Kata Tjuta National Park," 2017, parksaustralia.gov.au/uluru/ discover/history/.

6 Parks Australia, "Please Don't Climb Uluru," 2017, parksaustralia.gov.au/uluru/discover/culture/uluru-climb/.

7 Anna Codrea-Rado, "A Night in the Club, Then Early to Bed," *New York Times*, February 9, 2023.

8 Anna Codrea-Rado, "What Tweak Would Make Your Life Better?" A-Mail, February 17, 2023, annacodrearado.substack.com/p/one-small-tweak-thread.

9 M. Mahdi Roghanizad and Vanessa K. Bohns, "Ask in Person: You're Less Persuasive than You Think over Email," *Journal of Experimental Social Psychology* 69 (March 2017): 223–26.

10 Vanessa Bohns, "A Face-to-Face Request Is 34 Times More Successful Than an Email," *Harvard Business Review*, April 11, 2017.

CHAPTER 15: LET'S (ACTUALLY) GET TOGETHER SOMETIME

1 E. Kross et al., "Social Rejection Shares Somatosensory Representations with Physical Pain," *Proceedings of the National Academy of Sciences* 108, no. 15 (March 28, 2011): 6270–75.

CHAPTER 16: EXPRESSING APPRECIATION AND SUPPORT THE RIGHT WAY

1   Cleveland Clinic, "Dopamine: What It Is, Function & Symptoms," March 23, 2022.

2   Adelle X. Yang and Oleg Urminsky, "The Smile-Seeking Hypothesis: How Immediate Affective Reactions Motivate and Reward Gift Giving," *Psychological Science* 29, no. 8 (June 19, 2018): 1221–33.

CHAPTER 17: HOW TO BE CARING AND CURIOUS

1   Justin Theroux, interview with Jason Bateman, Will Arnett, and Sean Hayes, *SmartLess*, June 14, 2021, podcasts.apple.com/it/podcast /smartless/id1521578868.

2   Kat Vellos, *We Should Get Together: The Secret to Cultivating Better Friendships* (Katherine Vellos, 2020), 263–84.

3   Debra Fine, *The Fine Art of Small Talk: How to Start a Conversation, Keep It Going, Build Networking Skills, and Leave a Positive Impression!* (New York: Hachette Books, 2014), 29–31.

CHAPTER 18: TAMING YOUR INNER YODA

1   Michael Schaerer et al., "Advice Giving: A Subtle Pathway to Power," *Personality and Social Psychology Bulletin* 44, no. 5 (January 23, 2018): 746–61.

2   Leigh Plunkett Tost, Francesca Gino, and Richard P. Larrick, "Power, Competitiveness, and Advice Taking: Why the Powerful Don't Listen," *Organizational Behavior and Human Decision Processes* 117, no. 1 (January 2012): 53–65.

About the Author

A nna Goldfarb is a friendship journalist whose reporting has appeared in the *New York Times*, *The Atlantic*, Vox, Vice, the *Washington Post*, The Cut, *Time* magazine, and more. Called the "*New York Times* friendship correspondent" by Tim Herrera, editor of the *New York Times*' Smarter Living section, Goldfarb has written hundreds of articles that explore the nuances of friendships, relationships, and pop psychology. Anna's pieces about maintaining and rekindling friendships were excerpted in the *New York Times*' compilation book *Smarter Living: Work - Nest - Invest - Relate - Thrive*.

In 2012, Anna wrote the memoir *Clearly I Didn't Think This Through* (Berkley Books), born out of her humorous dating blog *Shmitten Kitten*, before pivoting to her career in journalism. She holds a BA in sociology from Barnard College, Columbia University, and an MA in journalism from Temple University. She lives in Philadelphia with her husband, Mike, and their tripawd cat, Eleanor.

About Sounds True

Sounds True was founded in 1985 by Tami Simon with a clear mission: to disseminate spiritual wisdom. Since starting out as a project with one woman and her tape recorder, we have grown into a multimedia publishing company with a catalog of more than 3,000 titles by some of the leading teachers and visionaries of our time, and an ever-expanding family of beloved customers from across the world.

In more than three decades of evolution, Sounds True has maintained our focus on our overriding purpose and mission: to wake up the world. We offer books, audio programs, online learning experiences, and in-person events to support your personal growth and awakening, and to unlock our greatest human capacities to love and serve.

At SoundsTrue.com you'll find a wealth of resources to enrich your journey, including our weekly *Insights at the Edge* podcast, free downloads, and information about our nonprofit Sounds True Foundation, where we strive to remove financial barriers to the materials we publish through scholarships and donations worldwide.

To learn more, please visit SoundsTrue.com/freegifts or call us toll-free at 800.333.9185.

Together, we can wake up the world.